CW00631498

Arthur's™

World of Cats

Arthur's

World of Cats

ANN HEAD

MAIN PHOTOGRAPHS BY GEOFF WILKINSON
ADDITIONAL PHOTOGRAPHY BY MARC HENRIE

Lennard Publishing

ACKNOWLEDGEMENTS

'Arthur' appears in this book by kind permission of
Dalgety Spillers Foods Limited with whom he is under exclusive contract.

Many thanks to the following for their help in providing information and additional photographs:
Penny Akehurst, Chiaro Burmese; Lynda Ashmore, Kralahome Cats (Devon Rex); The Balinese Cat Club;
David Brinicombe, Keoka Maine Coons; British Film Institute; Daphne Butters, Maine Coon Cat Club;
Bob Cooper, Bruvankedi Turkish Vans; Angela Crowther, Angisan Cats (Siamese); Larry and Anne Gilbert, Fyskez Cats
(Russian Blue); The Governing Council of the Cat Fancy; Joyce and Frank Grieve, Agincourt Chinchillas; Bob Head ;
Jane Hellman (Manx); Angela McCaig; John Higgins and Andrea Moss, Volsung Norwegain Forest Cats;
Mrs Lillian Howard, Soleil Cats (Balinese); Rosemary Lowen, Wenlo Somalis; Mirror Group Newspapers;
Ogilvy & Mather (Elmlea); Sue Parslow; Angela Patmore; Popperfoto; Pat and Mike Randles; Rex Features;
Russell Fine Art; Kim Sayer; The Somali Cat Club; Spillers Petfoods; Amanda Thomas, Amoracoon Maine Coons;
June Tomkinson, Chevine Burmese; Trevor Turner,; Russian Blue Breeders Association; Gordon and Madeleine Whittaker
(Ragdoll); Mrs C Wooller, Rimana Cats (Havana and Oriental), *Your Cat* magazine.

A special thank you to Jill Martin, Welmar British Shorthairs, for her help and hospitality, and an extra special thank you
to all the cats and their owners who participated in the main photography.

The prayer on page 76 was translated from an old Russian prayer book by Ian Deverit-Bennett and is
reprinted from *The Russian Blue Breeders Association Handbook* by kind permission of the president
Trevor Turner, BVetMed, MRCVS.

First published in 1995 by
Lennard Publishing
a division of Lennard Associates Limited
Mackerye End, Harpenden, Hertfordshire AL5 5DR

Text © 1995 Ann Head

All rights reserved. No part of this publication may be reproduced, stored in a retrieval system, or
transmitted, in any form or by any means without the prior permission in writing of the publisher,
nor be otherwise circulated in any form of binding or cover other than that in which it is published
without similar condition including this condition being imposed on the subsequent purchaser.

A catalogue entry is available from the British Library

ISBN 1 85291 126 3

Design by Paul Cooper Design
Editors: Roderick Brown and Chris Hawkes
Reproduction by Global Colour
Production consultants: Reynolds Clark Associates
Printed and bound in Spain

CONTENTS

THE PHOTOGRAPHS

I have never had so much fun from any job before. It must have been at least four or five years ago that I had the notion to photograph cats in background which reflected their origins, and I had discussed the possibilities of producing a calendar along these lines for Spillers, and 'Arthur', but somehow we just didn't get around to it at the time. However, better late than never; and now we have produced a book... and a calendar as well! So it was worth the wait.

Geoff Wilkinson and I talked at length about the backgrounds, and we spent several weeks searching out suitable props. The Maine Coon, for example, is sitting on a 'jetty' made by my assistant Gary out of old planking. Geoff supplied the rope, and I found the anchor in my loft. As for the Devon Rex, if any reader works for the Department of Health and Hygiene please allow us a bit of artistic licence! We racked our brains to think of a suitable prop, and a Devon cream tea was considered the most appropriate. Actually the little cat totally ignored everything on the set in favour of a feather on a stick! So at the end of the shoot we had a pot of tea and ate the lot! The Russian Blue looks very regal with his Cossack jacket and hat, and the Siamese and Balinese look stunning with their oriental lilies, and orchids. We know the Havana does not really come from Cuba, but who cares? He looks grand with his box of cigars, so there we are.

I sincerely hope that this book will be enjoyed in the spirit in which it is intended. As a tribute to cats – all cats, posh and plain – where would we be without them?

FOREWORD

I have lived with cats for most of my life, and for the past eighteen years I have also had the privilege of working with them. Privilege is the only word to use: no cat will co-operate with anyone who wishes it to perform a specific act unless it has a mind to do so. Dogs (albeit for their own good) spend their entire lives restricted to the confines of their homes and gardens and to the length of a lead, with freedom only allowed as and when their owners consider it appropriate and safe. Society deems this responsible pet ownership. Horses will obligingly accept loads on their backs as they gallop around in circles jumping over fences whilst being controlled by bridle and bit. To impose any such restrictions upon a cat would be unthinkable: although a few will willingly walk on leads for short periods, the majority are free spirits. Independence is their charm. No one may dominate or master a cat – it simply would not tolerate the situation.

There are documented cases of dogs starving on their masters' graves out of devotion to duty, but if a cat is hungry all his 'loyalties' will disappear – he will simply go off in search of food, and if the bill of fare is better next door he is quite likely to move in. To 'train' a cat requires infinite patience and an understanding that, in order to get the animal to co-operate, one must first let it feel in charge of the situation. In other words that it has the trainer well and truly under control, and by performing the required behaviour, it will get an appropriate reward. A cat will co-operate only if it is worth his while. And don't imagine that one may obtain results by starving the animal – 'Arthur' would certainly not dip his paw daintily into his can if he were extremely hungry, he would simply knock it over and try any means to get at the contents. Infinite patience and gentle handling is the key.

Cats come in many shapes, colours and coat textures, pure breeds from all over the world with origins going back through the mists of time and some more recently created by man, all with their own fascinating characteristics. Domestic cats (mixed breeds) carry traits from many or possibly most of them. The choice is endless. This book has been compiled as a tribute to Arthur. He has enriched our lives and become a legend in his own lifetime.

ARTHUR'S STORY

He doesn't have a mean thought in his head and endears himself to everyone.

I have lost count of the number of times I have been asked to describe 'Arthur's' disposition, but the answer has always been the same: 'Quite simply, he's a gentleman.'

He doesn't have a mean thought in his head and endears himself to everyone. He simply strolls in to greet visitors, rubbing around legs and jumping up onto laps with his motor running. Amazingly, his behaviour is identical when he meets other animals – unafraid, it seems, of anything or anyone and quietly confident with his surroundings, he takes everything in his stride. It was this incredible temperament which drew me to him in the first place. I had recently returned from the USA, having spent six and a half years working in the studios in Los Angeles as assistant to Frank Inn, owner and trainer of the famous little dog 'Benji', the star of several major movies. During that time I had the good fortune to work on movies, TV specials, sit coms and commercials featuring a varied selection of animals owned by Frank, including, of course, domestic cats!

Upon my return I began to build a career back home in England and while my little dog 'Pippin' (a gift from Frank and a granddaughter of 'Benji'), was in quarantine, I acquired several more cats and dogs and started to train. It didn't take me long to pick up the threads and soon I was shooting commercials again. On the strength of this work and the experience I had acquired in the USA, Spillers Foods commissioned me in 1986 to find and train an 'Arthur Number 2'. The original cat had died in 1976, in dignified retirement at the grand old age of fifteen. I was honoured, but unsure that I would be able to find a cat with both the looks and temperament to fit the bill.

I did a nationwide search over a period of two months, and came up with nothing. I had many offers from people willing to loan or rent their cats to me, but no one was prepared to part with their pet on a permanent basis – and who could blame them? It is essential for a working animal of 'Arthur's' calibre to live with his trainer in order to build up a trusting relationship which will carry into the studios. A stranger taking them away, even for the odd day's shoot, is to say the least unsettling; furthermore, the responsibility upon the handler is enormous. No, I had to find a cat who would live with me. Eventually, in desperation, I called a good friend, Angela Patmore, who suggested that I try the Wood Green Animal Shelter in Heydon in Hertfordshire; there she is well known and could vouch for my suitability as a caring adopter. Angela Thomas, in charge of cats at the Shelter, showed me several whites, all beautiful, but wrong for one reason or another – too oriental-looking, too timid and so on. I asked if she could show me anything else. 'There's only one,' she replied, 'and I doubt if you would want him. He is in the hospital wing and very sick.'

I was rapidly running out of time so I asked to see him. He looked pathetic. He had lost all interest in grooming himself, was sickly and sniffly and covered in eczema. He was a picture of abject misery, and his eyes were so mucused it was impossible to tell their colour. The girls at the Shelter were doing their utmost to restore him to health, but with so many cats and dogs to care for, they could only give limited individual attention. 'Snowy' as he was then called was getting more than his share, indeed one of the girls, Jill McDermott, had even taken him home for a short spell in the hope that the extra TLC would speed his recovery. (Such is the dedication of the Wood Green staff that this situation is far from rare.) Now back in the hospital 'Snowy' needed a home, but who in their right mind would consider such a case? Now I am not particularly noted for being sound in mind; I said I was willing to take him.

It is not the Shelter's policy to part with sick animals under normal circumstances, but after consultation with the vet, it was decided that the cat was so seriously ill (and he was, believe me!) he could only benefit from individual attention. His chances of survival at that time were pretty low, but there was something very special about 'Snowy' even in his dreadful state – I just had a gut feeling that my search was over. I will never know exactly why I was prepared to take on what proved to

'Arthur' with some of his celebrity friends.

be an uphill struggle, but his sweet loving nature and calm placid disposition were obvious, in spite of his dreadful condition. Once we got him home, we took him to the vet immediately. He was found to be infested with parasites and worms, malnourished, and suffering from an eye infection, ear mites, a nasty cold and eczema. The vet told me that I was mad to take him on: 'For Heaven's sake don't let him get anywhere near your other cats.'

The next few weeks were quite a strain. 'Snowy' (as he was still being called) was isolated in the spare room, he was being treated several times during the day and night with various medications and had to endure an anti-parasitic shampoo. When his eyes were bathed I discovered that they were a stunning emerald green. We had a litter of pedigree British Blue kittens at the time, and I had to sterilise my hands and completely change my clothes whenever I went to feed the mother and babies – it was little short of a nightmare. Now when I look back over the past years I know that all the effort was worthwhile. As he improved 'Snowy' gradually regained his appetite followed by weight, and was eventually introduced to his product, 'Kattomeat'. He loved it once and after a few more weeks he took to training like a duck takes to water. He is amazingly intelligent and soon learned to sit like a dog.

Obviously he had to learn 'Arthur's' trademark – the paw in the can. Many cats eat from a can with their paws because their heads are too big to fit inside, but most walk around in the process or stand as they eat. We needed a cat to sit still! 'Snowy' was soon sitting behind the product in the perfect position and eating beautifully with his left paw (his predecessor had been left handed, too!). I had decided not to add to his original stress by causing confusion over his name too soon, but eventually, when I felt that he was feeling sufficiently secure, I changed his name to 'Arthur'. The job complete at last, 'Arthur' was launched to the press at the Savoy Hotel on 11 January 1987.

He performed superbly, sitting and taking in all the attention from the photographers and visitors. Flash bulbs didn't bother him in the least. I was so proud of him that I found it hard to control the lump in my throat. Since then he has gone from strength to strength. He now makes commercials every year, and in addition he works on photo sessions and makes press and personal appearances. He also attends schools and old peoples homes, and regularly visits the National Cat Show at Olympia, where his stand draws in huge crowds of visitors. He receives cards and letters from people of all ages. I honestly feel he loves every moment of his lifestyle. Anyone who has visited him at the Shows will vouch for his relaxed composed attitude, basking in all the attention. What a pro! We love him dearly. He has been a very important part of our family for almost ten years, and when he eventually retires I am certain that he will still quite happily jump into his box to join in the fun at the occasional pensioners' Christmas party. Like Frank Sinatra, old troopers never give up completely. Over the past years his image has steadily grown in stature so much so that in 1992

'Kattomeat' was re-named 'Arthur's', a fitting tribute to his popularity.

'Arthur' is a super cat to live with. He is not in the least destructive, and I have never known him sharpen his claws on anything other than his scratching post. Very placid and easy-going, he loves to sit with us in the evenings when we are watching TV. Sometimes he shares 'Pippin's' basket, but more often than not he drapes himself over the arm of one of the easy chairs and hangs like a cheetah.

He looks remarkably good for his age. I don't know exactly how old he is but he has been living with us for almost ten years and was an adult cat when we adopted him, so he must at least qualify for a bus pass in human terms! Even though we don't know his actual date of birth, like the Queen he has an *official* birthday, celebrated in December. Like many of us (myself included), he has to watch his waistline these days. He has an amazing appetite and adores his own product which is his staple diet. I have to confess that I do sometimes succumb to his little tricks (he can, of course, beg like a dog), and if no one is looking give him the occasional cat treat.

Arthur has his very own chaise longue presented to him by Spillers who organise the Arthur's Awards held annually at BAFTA. He loves it and it always impresses visitors when they see him lounging on it.

'Arthur' visits his vet Tim Davies, of the Nine Mile Veterinary Hospital, Wokingham, for a routine check-up.

THE WOOD GREEN ANIMAL SHELTER, HEYDON

Where it all began... for 'Arthur' and many thousands of other lost, abused and neglected animals of all kinds. If there hadn't been a Wood Green Animal Shelter, I'd never have found that perfect white cat, and millions of us would have never known those wonderful adverts with the great white star and his sometimes unruly friends!

But there's obviously a more serious side to my wanting to tell you about Wood Green and its activities. No one buying this book can fail to know that, sadly, this country abandons thousands of animals each year. And then there are those who are victims of cowardly cruelty. I say cowardly for who but a coward would take it out on any creature who is vulnerable and dependent?

'Arthur' at home shortly after his adoption.

Whatever the reason for their plight, animals in distress can find comfort and, hopefully, decent new homes at the Wood Green Shelters. But what's the story behind them?

The first shelter opened in Wood Green, north London (hence the name) in 1924. Concern for animals wasn't so widespread then and its early years were lean. Fortunately a dynamic and far-sighted woman, Dr Margaret Young, threw her energies into making the Shelter viable and the organisation has never looked back.

A major development was the acquisition in the 1950s of a run-down pigfarm at Heydon near Royston, on the Hertfordshire/Cambridgeshire borders. Heydon is a typical English village, tucked into gentle folds of the chalky countryside, and it's a tranquil spot to visit. But it's also the centre of a frantically busy team whose prime concern is the welfare of as many animals as possible.

Heydon's not the only Wood Green site. Shelter number three came into being in the late 1980s at Godmanchester near historic Huntingdon. It was opened by The Princess Royal and fittingly, was named after Dr Young in recognition of her groundbreaking work. In 1991 another Shelter in Evesham was acquired.

The London Shelter continues its work providing free treatment for animals whose owners have financial difficulties. It has other operations too, including a cat adoption scheme. At Heydon there are surgical facilities and rehoming programmes and even a gift and coffee shop – so go visit and spend your money in a good cause! The Godmanchester site, King's Bush Farm, is magnificent – 50 acres of paddocks in an idyllic rural setting. It too has a re-homing programme but you can also sponsor permanent residents to ensure their continued health and happiness. Again there are amenities for visitors and frequent special events, so try and keep an eye open for news of what's going on there!

In all the Shelters take in 13,000 animals each year and manage to re-home over 80% of them – what a brilliant achievement! The rest are either given permanent residency at the Shelters or, where appropriate, returned to the wild. And who pays for it? Animal lovers. It's not cheap. At the time of going to press the Shelter's veterinary fees alone were over £350,000 per annum. That's only one essential part of things. For the rest, I can't do better than quote from the Shelters' own brochure (produced in-house – no costly outwork here!):

Our recipe for success:
Step 1. Take 1 animal (rescued or brought for re-homing), add a full veterinary examination, innoculate for 1 year against a range of diseases, worm and place in an isolation unit. Stroke gently and feed for 1-2 weeks. Remove animal from unit and place in public view.
Step 2. Take 1 family (or other suitable person), discuss domestic situation, check out environment and if suitable, introduce to animal. If not, remove and start step 2 afresh.
Step 3. Neuter or spay animal if necessary, introduce to new home and check on progress from time to time.

What could be better? BUT – and there has to be a but – this procedure costs, on average, £141.34 (and that's based on 1993/4 expenditure – rest assured, it's probably more now). Wood Green Animal Shelters is a registered charity entirely dependent on public support. Please think about helping them – for 'Arthur's' sake and the sake of all the animals they care for.

Wood Green Animal Shelters
Heydon, Royston, Hertfordshire SG8 8PN
Tel: 01763 838329 Fax: 01763 838318

'Arthur' in his dressing room. Ann Head helps him to get ready for his very first commercial.

A Working Day

On a shoot day, 'Arthur' rises early. I usually turn on the light in his room at 5.30a.m. to stir him from his slumbers, and to ensure that he attends to his 'toiletries' in good time before his trip to the studio.

Meanwhile my assistant and I have tea and toast, do our checklist to make certain that nothing has been forgotten, and load the vehicle, ready for the journey – cat show people know the routine well.

At around 6.30a.m. 'Arthur' jumps into his travel cage and we set off. His cage is very large, and can accommodate a cat bed, drinking bowl and litter tray. He certainly travels in comfort! Obviously any animal

A selection of 'Arthur's' recent commercials. In the picture below a white kitten plays the role of young 'Arthur', as 'Arthur' himself watches a home movie of his childhood.

'Arthur' has a last look at the script with his director, John Perkins, and then (below) it's lights, camera, action!

dressing room, and give him a light breakfast. He is then left to rest and acclimatise for at least an hour. This gives us the opportunity to have something to eat ourselves from the crew breakfast bar. After that comes the routine chat with the director who will advise us of the precise action required, and any script changes which might have taken place overnight.

Depending how far advanced they are with the set and lighting, we may get the opportunity to read a morning paper before the 15-minute warning prior to shoot time. This vital quarter of an hour is always used for 'Arthur's' final grooming session. Then onto the set we go.

Each session before the camera is very short (say ten minutes or so) after which, if the set has to be re-lit, 'Arthur' will return to his dressing room for a rest; this can be anything from 20 minutes to an hour. And so the day goes on, following this pattern, with a break of one hour for everyone at lunch time. By around 5.00p.m. we are usually getting to the end of the working day, and 'Arthur', plus all his travelling equipment, is loaded up for the return journey. 'Arthur' is so *au fait* with the whole situation that he usually stretches, yawns, and dozes all the way home!

expected to perform in a studio environment should travel with the maximum of comfort and a minimum of stress.

Upon arrival we unload, settle 'Arthur' into his

ABYSSINIAN

THE MACHO CAT

Ancient Egyptian art depicted svelte, supple cats; these Egyptian cats are strikingly similar to present-day Abyssinians.

The Abyssinian is one of the world's oldest known breeds but there is some controversy as to its origins.

Ancient Egyptian art depicted svelte, supple cats, both in genre scenes of cats hunting and at play, and as lean elegant sculptures – one of the most beautiful is the bronze statuette of a cat representing the goddess Bastet, made around 600 BC and now in the British Museum. With their elegant muscular bodies, wedge-shaped heads, large ears bearing distinctive tufts at their tips, and their large almond-shaped eyes, these cats are strikingly similar to present-day Abyssinians.

Strangely, Ethiopia (formerly Abyssinia) is not thought to be their country of origin; more likely their ancestors lived in parts of South East Asia and along the coast of the Indian Ocean. Though any theory is impossible to prove, it is thought that they became domesticated and eventually found their way, probably via trade routes, to Abyssinia.

A stuffed cat in Leiden Museum in Holland, described as 'A Ruddy Ticked Cat', apparently acquired around 1834 and labelled 'Patre Domestica India', strengthens this theory as it closely resembles the Abyssinian as we know it.

The first cats of this type to enter England were probably introduced when soldiers returned from Sir Charles Napier's campaign in Abyssinia in 1868. A Mrs Barrett Lennard, the wife of an army captain, brought a cat back with her. 'Zula', named after the port where the expedition first landed, had the tell-tale, distinctive 'ticked' coat, and sleek elegance. In 1882 the Abyssinian was acknowledged as a breed, but already crosses with British cats had diluted the stock, and experts proposed the name 'Abyssinian type'. The characteristic ticking led to other names, and around 1900 they were

Foreign type of medium build, firm, lithe and muscular, never large or coarse. The head to be broad and tapering to a firm wedge set on an elegant neck. The body to be of medium length with fairly long tapering tail. A 'cobby' cat is not permissible.

Head *– A moderate wedge of medium proportions, the brow, cheeks and profile lines showing a gentle contour and the muzzle not sharply pointed. A shallow indentation forming the muzzle is desirable but a pinch is a fault. In profile the head shows a gentle rounding to the brow, with a slight nose break leading to a very firm chin.*

Ears *– Set wide apart and pricked, broad at base, comparatively large, well cupped and preferably tufted.*

Eyes *– Well apart, large, bright and expressive in an oriental setting. A squint is a fault. Colour, amber, hazel or green. A light eye colour is undesirable.*

Feet *– Small and oval.*

Tail *– Broad at base, fairly long and tapering. Neither a whip nor a kink is permissible.*

Coat *– Short, fine and close lying with double, or preferably, treble ticking, i.e. two or three bands of colour on each hair.*

Markings *– It is required that the appropriate darker hair colour extends well up the back of the hind legs; also showing as a solid tip at the extreme end of the tail, and the absence of either is a fault. A line of dark pigmentation is required round the eyes and the absence of this is also a fault. Undesirable markings are bars on the legs, chest and tail. An unbroken necklet is not permissible. The Abyssinian cat has a tendency to white in the immediate area of the lips and lower jaw and it is a fault if this white area extends on to the neck. A locket and other white markings are not permissible.*

During the preparation for this book I spoke to many people with Abys, and one factor came through loud and clear. Whilst Abyssinian cats are extremely popular with women, the breed genuinely appeals to men! As we well know, lots of husbands and partners accept and, to a greater or lesser degree, are affectionate towards their lady's cats, whatever the breed, but when asked if they were to choose a pedigree cat for themselves several said without hesitation the Abyssinian. Men seem to adore them.

The cat in the main picture on the previous page is 'Koperkat Griffin' – 'Stef'.

Katelijne Vandamme is a vet practising in Warwickshire. She and her husband Kurt share their home with two Abyssinians: 'Stef' and his brother 'Koperkat Gus'. 'Stef' and 'Gus' are a bit like Laurel and Hardy – they seem to drift from one disaster to another (in the nicest way of course!). 'Stef' is by far the worse and Katelijne has her work cut out keeping tabs on him. Naturally curious (in fact to be honest, a nosy parker) 'Stef' will think nothing of strolling down the road until he finds an open door – then he goes into the house, takes a jolly good look around every room upstairs and

Katelijne Vandamme with 'Stef'.

called 'British Ticks', 'Ticks' and, less elegantly, 'Bunny Cats'. The founding of the Abyssinian Cat Club in 1929 established standards for the breed that continue, in essence, today.

Abyssinians are almost dog-like in their mannerisms. They will follow at one's heels all over the house and garden. Chatty but not too noisy, superbly intelligent and trainable, they can be trained to adapt to the family routine and will soon learn to come when called. They expect any requests to be worth their while and no Aby owner should be without a pocket full of treats.

Right and opposite page: Abyssinian kittens on the prowl.

down, then leaves again. By now the neighbours have got used to these impromptu visits and just accept that if they hear a noise upstairs, it is probably 'Stef' on the prowl again. On one such visit he disgraced himself by breaking a piece of irreplaceable china on the bay

'Stef' and 'Gus' are great hunters – like all Abys – and 'Stef' has often brought home a catch to present to Katelijne: shock horror, fish from the neighbour's pond! He also recently stole a bone from a local dog and managed to drag it into his own garden, only to get it

windowsill of a lady who lives down the road. He arrived home in a bit of a hurry with a guilty look on his face and the irate neighbour in hot pursuit, so I suppose he could be described as a 'smashing' cat. Both

stuck in the cat flap. Nowhere is safe from 'Stef'. Both he and 'Gus' are adored by their owners and although beautifully bred, they are not exhibited at cat shows. They just live happily as family pets.

BALINESE

A SIAMESE WITH FRINGES

The breed evolved in the USA in the mid 1950s when Siamese to Siamese matings produced occasional long-haired kittens.

*J*ust as the Somali is a semi-long-haired version of the Abyssinian Cat, so the Balinese is a Siamese with a long, silky coat. The breed evolved in the USA in the mid 1950s when Siamese to Siamese matings produced occasional long-haired kittens. The attractive offspring had delightful personalities and breeders soon tried mating long-haired Siamese to long-haired Siamese. The surprising outcome was that the kittens were always born true to type.

This proved that the long-haired cats carried only long-haired genes, whereas the short-haired traditional Siamese carried both. As a result, breeders were able to produce these beautiful cats in sufficient numbers to create a new breed, the Balinese. Why Balinese? There is no real connection with the island of Bali, although we have used a bit of creative licence with our photograph, suggesting by the sea shells that our model cat is sunning himself on a beautiful beach in the South Seas.

The name actually stemmed from a chance remark by a breeder, Mrs Helen Smith of New York, who described the movement of these cats as akin to the grace of Balinese dancers. The name Balinese was readily accepted by all, as it so aptly describes these attractive creatures; and from those early days the breed has gone on from strength to strength.

The first Balinese to come to England were imported in 1973 – a male cat and his daughter. The female was pregnant, and produced a litter of four kittens in quarantine. These cats came into the hands of Mrs Sandra Bird of Sussex and were the ancestors of today's English Balinese Cats.

The Balinese cat should be a beautifully balanced animal, with head, ears and neck carried on a lithe and graceful body, supported on slim legs and feet, with the tail in proportion and with a medium long coat, fine and silky in texture. The head and profile should be wedge-shaped, neither round nor pointed; the mask complete, connected by tracings with the ears (except in kittens); the eyes a clear bright blue, expression alert and intelligent.

Head – *Long and well proportioned, carried upon an elegant neck, with width between the ears, narrowing in perfectly straight lines to a fine muzzle, with straight profile, strong chin and level bite.*

Ears – *Rather large and pricked, with width at base. The ears may be tufted.*

Eyes – *Oriental in shape and slanting towards the nose, but with width between. Colour bright, clear blue and complimentary to points colour.*

Body, Legs and Feet – *Body medium in size, lithe and graceful. Legs proportionately slim, hind legs slightly higher than front legs; feet small and oval. The body, legs, feet and tail should all be in proportion, giving the whole a well balanced appearance.*

Tail – *Long and tapering and free from any kink.*

Points – *Mask, ears, legs, feet and tail dense with colour clearly defined, matching on all points, showing clear contrast between points and body colour. Mask complete (except in kittens) connected by tracings with the ears.*

Note: *As coat length tends to disguise tail markings on Tabby Point and Tortie Point cats, the tail should be held by the tip, shaken and viewed from the rear.*

Coat – *Medium-long, fine and silky in texture, without woolly undercoat, lying mainly flat along the body; tail plume-like.*

The Balinese is a picture of grace and elegance, an enchanting creature with a delightful personality. These cats make wonderful pets, they are lively and amusing and will find fun with a champagne cork or a humble bit of screwed up paper. String and balls of wool provide hours of amusement. Very people orientated, these cats will drape themselves around their owners' shoulders or follow them from room to room like pretty little dogs.

The cat in the main picture on the previous page is 'Grand Champion Lookame Simply Red' – 'Fred'.

Bred and owned by Brenda Kennell of Warwickshire, three-years-old 'Simply Red' was originally named after his owner's favourite pop group. It seemed very appropriate at the time as he was born a reddish kitten, but as he got older, 'Fred' grew gradually lighter until he became cream in colour. He has now gone on to become a Grand Champion in the show ring. Brenda says that 'Fred' is a great big softie. Very loving and chatty, 'Fred' has a passion for white meat and Brenda will leave a plate of cold chicken within his reach at her peril. 'Fred' is very graceful and elegant, but prone to breaking into sudden bursts of activity, just to keep Brenda on her toes. He will think

nothing of treating the living room, open window and patio as his own Brands Hatch circuit, dashing round and round, in through the door and out again through the open window. Life is never dull with 'Fred' around, but at the end of a summer day he will probably be found basking in the warm evening sun, a picture of peace and tranquillity. This doesn't fool Brenda for a moment and she wouldn't have it any other way! Brenda is married to Tom Kennell, who owns 'Penny', our lovely Lilac Siamese pictured on page 81.

Editor of the Balinese Cat Club Magazine Norman Webb and his wife Sheila own four Balinese who go everywhere with them, even on holiday. The Webbs own a caravan and the cats are never left behind. Excellent travellers, they go for miles during the summer season and love every minute of it.

Above: Tom Kennell and 'Fred'.
Left: Norman and Sheila Webb's Balinese enjoying life on the road.
Right above: Mum (in the background) keeps a watchful eye on her sleeping family.
Right: 'Percy', a five-month-old seal Balinese relaxes at home.

BIRMAN

According to legend these cats were once pure white and were the guardians of the goddess Tsun-Kyan-Kse.

Birmans are cats of exceptional beauty. The development of the breed is a mystery. According to legend, these cats were once pure white and were guardians of the statue of the goddess Tsun-Kyan-Kse in the Lao-Tsun Temple in ancient Burma. The statue was of pure gold with brilliant sapphires for eyes. The cats lived with the priests of the Khmer people and were held in high regard both for their exceptional beauty and their devotion to duty.

The priests were often persecuted, and one day the temple was raided by vandals intent on stealing the holy treasures. On discovering their presence the High Priest ran to protect the sacred statue, but before he could reach it he was attacked. As he lay dying one of the temple cats sat in vigil by his side, her heart breaking at the sight of her beloved master. She placed her front feet gently on his head to comfort him and, as his last breath passed away, the spirit of the statue passed into her body. Her coat turned from pure white to pale gold and her eyes became sapphire blue. Shadows from the ground settled on her face, but her feet, which were still resting on her dead master's head, remained pure snow white. The white 'gloves', gentle blue eyes, and shadowy face have remained with Birmans from that day onwards.

Grace Pond's *The Complete Cat Encyclopedia* relates that the temple was threatened at the turn of this century; fortunately two foreigners named Auguste Pavie and Major Gordon Russell assisted the priests and were later sent two Birman cats to their home in France as a mark of gratitude. Sadly the male died on the long journey but the female, who was pregnant, survived and her kittens founded the breed as we know it. The development was slow, but in the UK the GCCF awarded them Championship Status in 1966. These cats are exquisite. They are wise and gentle, good with

Head – *Skull strong, broad and rounded. Nose medium in length (no 'stop' but with slight dip in profile). Cheeks full and round. Chin full and well developed, slightly tapered but not receding.*

Ears – *Medium in size and spaced well apart.*

Eyes – *Almost round but not bold. Blue in colour; the deeper the blue the better.*

Body – *Long and massive.*

Legs and Paws – *Legs of medium length and thick-set; paws short and strong.*

Tail – *Bushy. Medium in length and in proportion to body.*

Coat and Condition – *Coat long, silken in texture; full ruff around neck; slightly curled on the stomach. The cat should be well grown, the frame (skeleton) should be strong, well covered and muscular. Eyes bright and temperament good.*

Coat and Condition – *The distinguishing colours of the Birman are those of the Siamese. Mask, ears, legs and tail dense and clearly defined (except in kittens). On reaching maturity, the mask covers the whole face including whisker pads and is connected to the ears by tracings.*
Note: *Body shading in points colour in Provisional status adults is allowed but good contrast must remain.*
White feet are characteristic of the Birman:

Front Paws – *Have pure white symmetrical gloves ending in an even line across the paw and not passing beyond the angle formed by the paw and leg. Colour of the paw pads irrelevant.*

Back Paws – *Have pure white gloves (gauntlets) covering the entire paw and tapering up the back of the leg to finish just below the point of the hock. Colour of the paw pads is irrelevant.*

A bluepoint Birman relaxes in the garden.

children and have a calming influence on everyone they meet. Owning a Birman is said to help with the relief of stress.

The cat in the main picture on the previous page is 'Sandatal Amber' – 'Lao'.

Three-year-old 'Lao' is a 'Seal Point Birman' and lives in Warwickshire with his owners Maureen and Roy Fall, together with 'Simba', the delightful young Oriental Cinnamon featured on page 69 and a second Birman, 'Kyan'.

All three cats have the run of the house and garden, entering and leaving through a cat flap in the integral garage door. Maureen and Roy have 'cat-proofed' their garden in such a way that 'Lao' and co. cannot escape. They erected short posts extending from the top of their fence at intervals and joined them together with soft wire netting. Then they fixed an overhang of fine wire mesh all around the top, hanging loosely into their own garden. This apparently makes it impossible for the home cats to climb out, and what is even more important, it prevents visiting cats from getting in. Ingenious! Not that 'Lao', 'Kyan' and little 'Simba' are in the least deprived by being confined to their garden. They have lots of room inside and out and have a super time chasing each other up and down the trees. Birmans are not renowned for their climbing abilities but 'Lao' is particularly adept at it, especially when he needs to

Above: Roy Fall with 'Lao'.
Above right: The unusual sight of a Birman at the seaside.
Below: Kittens in mittens.

get out of the house in a hurry, and out of Maureen's reach. He was recently to be seen dashing down the garden with one of his 'prizes' – the pork chop intended for Roy's supper! 'Lao' is a loveable rogue. If there is any mischief afoot one may rest assured that he has probably had some hand (paw) in it.

Like most Birmans 'Lao' is very good natured, and he has perfected the knack of endearing himself to Maureen in the wake of mischief. He still acts like a naughty kitten, which adds to his charm.

'Lao' is not as vocal as a Siamese cat, but like all Birmans he is very 'talkative' and can be persistent when meal times come around. A home lover, 'Lao' has never been to a cat show as it seems that his 'white mittens' are not quite long enough (in fact the judges would say that they are much too short) but who cares about that! As Maureen says, 'What he lacks in mittens he makes up for in character!'

BRITISH SHORTHAIR

They were most likely brought to England on ships during the Roman invasion.

As with many breeds, the background of these cats is uncertain. They were most likely brought to England on ships during the Roman invasion.

These tough, substantial, short-haired cats were probably sought after, as they would have been easy to keep, long-lived and hardy. Shorthairs are fine hunters, and these cats would have been prized as rat catchers.

Round-headed, sturdy and stocky, alert and predatory, these ancient felines are probably the ancestors of the British Shorthairs as we know them today. Natural selection would have meant the survival of the fittest, the thick, dense, plush coats developing as protection against inclement weather.

In time a variety of colourations appeared, spots and stripes being amongst them, probably inherited from the African wildcat. These cats survived in the domestic environment for hundreds of years until eventually breeders took a hand in their development, refining the coarser points and enhancing the more significant features. The round 'apple face' is now synonymous with the breed, as is the cobby appearance and the thick, slightly coarse coat.

At the earliest English cat shows in the 1800s, shorthairs greatly outnumbered the longhairs, but this situation was to change at the turn of the century.

The British Shorthair Cat Club was formed in 1901. The subscription was five shillings, and in the early days the most popular types were tabbies, whites and black and whites. Today there is a considerable choice in patterns, and colouration ranging from black to white, tabbies, spotties and plains in striking shades. The most popular is the plain-coated British Blue.

These cats are gentle and quiet and very good with children. Excellent at grooming themselves, they require very little help from their owners. A simple brush

---

The British cat is compact, well balanced and powerful, showing good depth of body, a full broad chest, short strung legs, rounded paws, tail thick at base with rounded tip. The head is round with a good width between small ears, round cheeks, firm chin, large round and well-opened eyes and a short broad nose. The coat is short and dense. A muscular cat with an alert appearance and in perfect physical condition.

Head – Round face with full cheeks and good breadth of skull with round underlying bone structure. The head should be set on a short thick neck.

Nose – The nose itself should be short, broad and straight. In profile, a rounded forehead should lead to a short, straight nose with a nose break which is neither too pronounced nor too shallow.

Chin – A strong, firm and deep chin is essential. The bite must be level, the tip of the chin to line up with the tip of the nose in the same vertical plane.

Ears – Small, rounded at the tips, set far apart fitting into (without distorting) the rounded contour of the head. External ear to be well covered with fur, internal furnishings not to be excessive.

Eyes – Large, round and well opened. Set wide apart with no tendency to Oriental shape. No squint.

Body – Cobby type with short level back. Low on legs with broad deep chest. Equally massive across the shoulders and the rump. Medium to large, but not rangy.

Legs and Paws – Short, strong legs. Paws round and firm. Toes carried close, five on each forefoot (including dew claw) and four on each back foot.

Tail – Should be thick and of medium length, thicker at the base with rounded tip.

Legs and Paws – Must be short, dense and crisp. A soft and/or over-long and fluffy coat is incorrect.

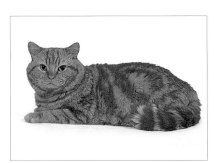

through the coat once or twice a week will suffice. They are home lovers, not prone to wandering, and are still excellent mousers to this day.

The cat in the main picture on the previous page is 'Kernmere Crescendo' – 'Cassie'.

'Cassie' belongs to Jill Martin from Warwickshire who has been breeding British Shorthairs for over ten years; her prefix 'Welmar' is now well known around the shows.

Jill is a musician, a teacher of music in fact, and several of her cats ('Cassie' in particular) are likewise musically inclined. There is nothing 'Cassie' likes better

Jill Martin has built up a fine reputation for showing British Shorthairs. She is currently working on a breeding programme experimenting with new and exciting colours. We picture one of her 'girls', 'Welmar Silver Secret' – 'Sylvie', who as one can see is a lovely silver tabby. She was recently mated to a plain chocolate coloured male, and has produced a veritable rainbow of kittens, one colour pointed, one plain chocolate (like Dad), two blacks (or possibly black smokes – at the time of the photo it was too soon to tell), one chocolate spotted, and (this is the exciting bit!) a chocolate tabby!

Jill thinks that this is one of the first, if not *the* first chocolate tabby British Shorthair to be born in the UK.

Above: Martyn Lewis with the tabby kittens produced by his British Silver Tabby, 'Rosie'.
Above right: Hera Cooper (left) with 'Harlequin' and Jill Martin with 'Pineapple Poll'.

than to take part in a good piano lesson; she joins in with gusto. As soon as the lid is raised, she jumps up on to the keyboard to add her interpretation to the piece. 'Cassie' is a typical British Blue, sweet-natured and beautiful. A gem to work with, I have featured her on several of my photo shoots, and she has always behaved impeccably.

The kitten, a female, has beautiful classic markings in a rich dark brown. It was a thrill to photograph such an important little lady! A mere five days old, she is history in the making. Jill also bred one of my own British Shorthairs, a lilac tabby, 'Welmar Busy Lizzie' – 'Possum', pictured opposite improving her chess game.

All British Shorthairs have stunning round eyes in colours ranging from pale gold to deepest copper. Over the years I have owned three of these cats and I have loved each one. They are hard to fault, long-lived, affectionate and loyal, with super looks.

Top: The inquisitive faces of three blue kittens.
Above: 'Possum' makes her move.
Above left: 'Sylvie' with her rainbow of kittens.
Left: 'Sylvie's' chocolate tabby kitten.

BURMESE

'Dr Thompson's Little Brown Cat' travelled with him to the USA from her native Rangoon.

'Wong Mau' is probably the grandmother of present-day Burmese cats. She was known as 'Dr Thompson's Little Brown Cat' and she had travelled with him to the USA from her native Rangoon in 1930. Joseph Thompson, a retired American ship's doctor with a particular interest in cats, had been visiting Burma at the time and although we do not know how 'Wong Mau' came into his possession we are pretty certain that she stayed with him for the rest of her life. We cannot be sure if the cat was pure bred; it is possible that she wasn't. She may have been a cross, now known as a Tonkinese (Tonkin was the name given to North Vietnam under French rule). Upon his return to the United States, Dr Thompson mated 'Wong Mau' to a Siamese male. Darker 'pointed' kittens were born; they were retained and bred together. Some of the offspring of this mating had distinct solid brown or sable coats, and they were probably the foundation stock of Burmese cats as we know them today. Between 1932 to 1940, several other American breeders joined forces with Dr Thompson to develop the breed further, gradually lessening the Siamese 'points'. Slowly but surely these self-coloured cats increased in numbers, and as they became more popular they began to appear on the American show benches. During that period several more cats were imported from Burma to the

The Burmese is an elegant cat of a foreign type, with characteristics quite individual to the breed. Any suggestions of either Siamese type, or the cobbiness of a British cat, must be regarded as a fault.

Head and Ears *– The head should be slightly rounded on top, with good breadth between the ears, having wide cheek bones and tapering to a short blunt wedge. The jaw should be wide at the hinge and the chin firm. A muzzle pinch is a bad fault. Ears should be medium in size, set well apart on the skull, broad at the base with slightly round tips, the outer line of the ears continuing the shape of the upper part of the face. This may not be possible in mature males who develop a fullness of cheek. In profile the ears should be seen to have a slight forward tilt. There should be a distinct nose break, and in profile the chin should show a strong lower jaw.*

Eyes *– Must be set well apart. They should be large and lustrous, the top line of the eye showing a straight oriental slant towards the nose, the lower line being rounded. Either round or oriental eyes are a fault.*

Eye Colour *– any shade of yellow from chartreuse to amber, with golden yellow preferred. Green eyes are a serious fault in Brown Burmese, but Blue Burmese may show a slight fading of colour. Green eyes with more blue than yellow pigmentation must preclude the award of a Challenge Certificate in Burmese of all colours.*

Body *– Of medium length and size, feeling hard and muscular, and heavier than its appearance indicates. The chest should be strong, and rounded in profile, the back straight from the shoulder to rump.*

Legs and Paws *– Legs should be slender and in proportion to the body; hind legs slightly longer than front; paws neat and oval in shape.*

Tail *– Straight and of medium length, not heavy at base, and tapering only slightly to a rounded tip without bone defect. A visible kink or other bone defect in the tail is a fault, precluding the award of a Challenge Certificate, but an invisible defect at the extreme tip may be overlooked in an otherwise excellent specimen.*

Coat *– The coat should be short, fine, satin-like in texture, lying close to the body. The glossy coat is a distinctive feature of Burmese and is indicative of good health.*

USA to enable breeders to introduce new bloodlines. Around 1953 the first Burmese cats appeared in England and experimentation with new colours was inevitable. In 1955 a silvery grey kitten was born (named 'Seal Coat Blue Surprise') and the breeding programme continued to progress. Eventually the brown Burmese was recognised by the GCCF in 1952 and the blue cats were shown in 1960.

Burmese cats are now very popular. Their temperament is excellent; outgoing, friendly and gregarious, they are natural retrievers and most will return a cat toy time and time again if it is thrown for their amusement. They are handsome creatures, elegant and proud with chartreuse yellow (or sometimes palish green) eyes. They now appear wearing coats of many attractive colours and there can be no doubt that they have come a long way since the days of Dr Thompson's 'Little Brown Cat'.

Left: Jill Kirkland and 'Buster'.
Below: Trouble in store – three kittens play in the kitchen cupboard.

The cat in the main picture on page 33 is 'Katawampuss Borage' – 'Buster.'

'Buster' is a two-year-old blue Burmese who lives with Jill and Simon Kirkland of Leicestershire. 'Buster's' sister 'Misha', a very elegant lilac Burmese, is also a much-loved member of the household. Very recently the family was made complete by the arrival of a baby son, Thomas. Until the birth of the baby, 'Buster' was a typical Burmese family pet, inquisitive, boisterous, sometimes naughty, always affectionate, and like his sister, constantly demanding attention.

He is still all of these things but now he has taken over a new role. He has become a protector! Fascinated with

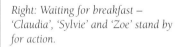

Above: 'Rotti', a sixteen-month-old Burmese, poses among the plants.

Right: Waiting for breakfast – 'Claudia', 'Sylvie' and 'Zoe' stand by for action.

Below: Bedtime for 'Spotcat', 'Cleopatra' and 'Sophie'.

Thomas, 'Buster' now spends most of his days just sitting like a cat on guard at the foot of the cradle. Jill keeps a cat net over the baby so there is no danger. 'Buster' simply does not want to leave and it seems that as Thomas grows up, he will have a constant companion. 'Buster' keeps himself amused by carrying a paper ball around in his mouth like a little dog. He is constantly dropping it at the feet of anybody who looks a likely prospect for a game of 'Toss and Fetch'. Visitors and family alike, 'Buster' will try his luck with anyone! It looks as though young Thomas will have a ready-made playmate, particularly when it comes to ball games!

CHINCHILLA

GLAMOUR PUSS

The original long-haired cats from Persia found their way into various countries via the Silk Route.

*I*t is a romantic and interesting theory that the original long-haired cats from Persia found their way into various countries via the Silk Route many hundreds of years ago, transported by traders. This is quite feasible. The Silk Route, originating in China, was a network of 'roads' along which Eastern luxuries – silk obviously, but jade, too – came to eastern Mediterranean ports. Fabled cities such as Samarkand, Bukhara and Merv all benefitted from it, as did Babylon and Baghdad. The civilizations in what is now Iran occasionally depicted long-haired cats in their illustrated manuscripts – so it is possible that valued felines were carried along the great treks. After all, a cat isn't a large item of baggage!

Whatever its earlier history, we can be certain that the Chinchilla strain started to develop in the nineteenth century – around 1880 long-haired Persian-type cats with distinct silver tabby markings started to appear. Probably the first was 'Silver Lambkin', who proved a sensation at contemporary cat shows, and who has been preserved at the Natural History Museum. It is hard to believe that these cats were (and still are) genetically black. They developed through selective breeding by producing lighter and lighter kittens and in the 1930s Chinchilla cats appeared in numbers. Thereafter the breed continued to evolve into the exquisite creature as we know it today. Basically pure white with silver tipping to the outer coat, the undercoat and chest hair must be unmarked and solid white, the outer hair long and lustrous like the silk from its supposed country of origin. Its faint tipping produces a silver sheen when caught in the sunlight. The eyes, large and luminous, are usually vivid emerald green, but may also be turquoise, and they appear to me to have kohl pencil liner around the rims.

If you buy a young kitten and it doesn't appear as pure white as its mother, don't be perturbed. The silver tabby markings sometimes evident in the babies will gradually fade and almost disappear with age, leaving the faint tipping which gives the adult cat its glamour. There are various depths of colour and any prospective kitten owner should ask the breeder about the background of the parents to ascertain (as well as one can) what colour one may expect the grown cat to be. Also there are new variations appearing including gold, so ask around or visit a show. Most breeders are delighted to offer help and advice.

Chinchillas make wonderful companions and are livelier than other Persians. They are great fun to own but they are cats requiring *time*. The coat requires regular gentle grooming to prevent knots and tangles forming. The very action of stroking an animal has been

---

Head and Ears – *Head broad and round, with breadth between ears, which should be small and well furnished; wide at the muzzle; snub nose.*

Eyes – *Large, round and most expressive, emerald or blue-green in colour.*

Body and Legs – *Cobby body; short thick legs.*

Tail – *Short and bushy.*

Coat and Condition – *Coat long and dense; silky and fine in texture; extra long on frill.*

Colour – *The undercoat pure and white, the coat on back, flanks, head, ears and tail being tipped with black; this tipping to be evenly distributed, thus giving the characteristic sparkling silver appearance. The legs may be very slightly shaded with the tipping, but the chin, ear furnishings, stomach and chest must be pure white; any tabby markings or brown or cream tinge is a defect. Nose leather brick-red, and visible skin on eyelids and the pads black or dark brown.*

*Above: Blofeld (Donald Pleasance), and his Chinchilla, with 007
(Sean Connery) in* You Only Live Twice.
*Right: Irene Doyle with one of her Chinchilla girls, 'Dreamer'.
Below right: Snooty 'Portia' makes her entrance.*

proved to be therapeutic and may relieve stress. So as
these cats *must be groomed regularly*, the time set aside
each day can be very beneficial for both cat and owner,
and the end result is certainly breathtaking. If you are
prepared to build up a close relationship with your pet
and dedicate at least half an hour a day to 'keeping up
appearances', then this chocolate box cat is for you!

Gladys Hayward-Barton has been respected in the
Chinchilla world for over twenty-five years and I
consider myself privileged to own one of her cats,
'Silcresta Madonna'. Our 'Donna' is now eleven years
old and reaching retirement and although she was never
shown, her fantastic temperament made her incredibly
easy to train. She has appeared in many commercials
over the years, and most recently could be seen as
'Portia' the snooty lady in the 'Elmlea' cream
commercials, together with my ginger moggie 'Harry'.
Gladys herself is not unknown to the film industry,
having supplied many cats and dogs through her
company known as Animal Casting. Remember
Blofeld's beautiful Chinchillas in the early James Bond
films?

*The cat in the main picture on the previous page is dual
champion (USA and UK) 'Dalee New Sensation'.*

Irene Doyle, prefix 'Iramajo', is the proud owner of
this beautiful boy. He was bred in San Diego California
and Irene brought him over to the United Kingdom
in July 1993. 'Sensation' was just eight months old at
the time and already a champion in his own country
– cats achieve championship status at a younger age
in the USA than in the UK. When his six months
quarantine were up, 'Sensation' settled into his new

Above: Mum with two glamour pussies of tomorrow.
Below: 'Susie' with 'Arthur' in the 'Sexy Eyes' commercial.

home and in no time at all was taking the United Kingdom show world by storm. Irene has been breeding and showing Chinchillas for ten years and 'Sensation' is making an excellent contribution to her already well respected bloodlines. He is quite a character, very laid back and placid, and being a natural poser he is a piece of cake to photograph. His favourite occupation is relaxing on the patio watching the birds feeding on Irene's garage roof. Being a cat lady she has more sense than to feed them on the ground.

'Sensation' shares his home with a German Shepherd, two Pekinese and an African grey Parrot – and guess who rules the roost!

While we're talking of Chinchillas, I can't miss this opportunity of sharing a delightful character with you, one who isn't a Chinchilla but Persian, and who makes a beautiful colour contrast to the snowiness of her close relations. Persian cats come in a variety of colours, the most popular probably being the blue. Blue Persians have always been associated with chocolate box lids and up-market calendars. They are without doubt beautiful creatures with wonderfully laid back affectionate temperaments.

One such is 'Suzie' the 'Alice blue gown' we used in the Arthur commercial 'Sexy Eyes'. 'Suzie' had never performed in front of TV cameras before, but on the day of the shoot she behaved impeccably, sashaying down the line of 'Arthur's' awards, and blinking straight into the camera at the required moment with her great big orange eyes – a perfect take!

DEVON REX

THE PIXIE CAT

A stray mother and kittens were found in a hedgerow near a tin mine in Buckfastleigh, Devon, which was a known haunt for local feral cats.

Rex Cats are not restricted to the United Kingdom. There are several types and they can be found in various parts of the world, from Oregon in the USA to Holland and Germany in Europe.

In England there are two distinct types. Both are curly coated but derive from two different mutant genes. Curly coated cats had been seen on Bodmin Moor, Cornwall on several occasions in the late 1940s, and in 1950 a short-haired farm cat called 'Serena' produced a litter of five kittens, one of which was a wavy coated male with curly whiskers. The general consensus of opinion was that this young boy had a similar coat to a Rex Rabbit. He was called 'Kallibunker' but I think 'Oedipus' would have been a more suitable name, as he was destined to be mated back to his own mother, and their offspring were the foundation of the Cornish Rex breed.

Now the story gets more interesting. In 1960 a stray mother and kittens were found in a hedgerow near a tin mine in Buckfastleigh, Devon, which was a known haunt for local feral cats. The little family was apparently discovered by a Miss Beryl Cox, who took them into her home and cared for them. It was a perfectly ordinary litter except for one male who had a short wavy coat. Fascinated by this tiny fellow, Miss Cox decided to keep him, finding homes for the rest. He grew into a delightful little cat and she named him 'Kirlee'. 'Kirlee' was devoted to Miss Cox and followed her everywhere almost like a small dog; he even wagged his tail!

Upon hearing of Rex Cats in Cornwall, which by then (ten years on) were becoming more plentiful, Miss Cox contacted a breeder and 'Kirlee' was eventually mated to a Cornish Queen, but the results of the union were disappointing. Flat coats all! Eventually it became plain that the Cornish Rex and the Devon Rex evolved from two different genes and it took some time to get the whole breeding programme established, but eventually other suitable queens appeared in both counties, and the two distinct types developed.

Devons are the smaller of the two, their eyes are round and their ears are large and bat-like. Some breeders would have liked to have called them the Butterfly Rex, because viewed from behind the ears do look remarkably like a butterfly. They have slightly coarser and curlier coats than the Cornish, and they

Head – Wedge shaped with face full cheeked. Short muzzle with strong chin and whisker break. Nose with a strongly marked stop. Forehead curving back to flat skull.

Ears – Large, set rather low, very wide at base, tapering to rounded tops and well covered with fine fur. With or without ear muffs.

Eyes – Wide set, large, oval shaped and sloping towards outer edge of ears. Colour in keeping with coat colour or, except in Si-Rex, chartreuse, green or yellow.

Body, Legs and Neck – Body hard and muscular, slender and of medium length, broad in chest, carried high on slim legs, with length of hind legs emphasized. Paws small and oval. Neck slender.

Tail – Long, fine and tapering, well covered with short fur.

Coat – Very short and fine, wavy, curly and soft, can have a rippled effect. Whiskers and eyebrows crinkled, rather coarse, and of medium length.

Colours – All coat colours acceptable.

Rolf Harris, a great cat lover, with his Devon Rex 'Beetle Baby'.

extremely mischievous. The Devon has a hard muscular body and a broad chest. Its legs are long and slim and the large ears and high cheekbones give it a distinctly impish expression.

Rex cats were officially recognised by the Governing Council in the 1960s and showing in the UK has steadily grown in popularity. In the USA they have been shown since the 1970s.

The cat in the main picture on the previous page is two-year-old 'Nobilero Shaydar Logothia' – 'Harriet'.

Described as a Black Smoke Devon Rex, 'Harriet' is owned by Ken and Val King of Warwickshire. She would really be better named 'Raffles', as she is a true cat burglar. She takes great delight in stealing bright

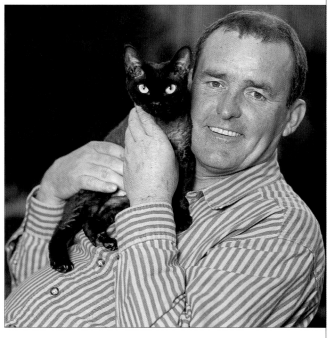

Ken King with 'Harriet'.

are often thinner and uneven. One source says neither the Cornish Rex nor the Devon Rex has an undercoat so they supposedly make better pets for people with allergies. The Devon coat will soak up water, and if these cats are left outside they must be given some shelter. The kittens are quite delightful pixie-like little creatures with wrinkled brows, and, some say, 'a face only a mother could love'! The Devon Rex has been nicknamed the 'Poodle Cat' because of its coat and also because the owners claim that they wag their tails when they are happy, like little dogs. They moult like most cats and their bodies can appear quite bald in places during the hot weather, especially on the underpart. This is probably due to the hair being finer there. When they are in their full winter coat they have wonderful waves on their backs, and when stroked the coat feels like thick plush. Some Devon Rex Cats have curly hair on the edges of their ears and these are known by the breeders as ear muffs. These do not appear in the breed standard but are not penalised in the Show Ring. Lovely lynxy tufts at the tips of the ears are preferred by many breeders. The whiskers of the Devon cats are quite brittle and occasionally get broken. They do not grow much and are often a little bit kinky. Rexes are loveable and lively family pets and, like pixies, they can be

objects which she actually takes in her mouth and hides in secret places. She has many such hideaways which are usually discovered when Val does her housework. A bit of screwed up kitchen foil turns up behind the sofa; a ring or small key is tucked away in a corner; a tiny pendant is found under a cushion. Anything small and bright is fair game.

Harriet has been with Val and Ken for two years and by now they are wise to her little tricks and keep everything of value under lock and key. Rex cats are affectionately described as the monkeys of the cat world, and there can be no doubt that life is never dull with one around the house. They do indeed climb – no curtain is safe! Like pet monkeys they will ride on shoulders for hours at a time. Gregarious in nature, they love all company but are very loyal to their owners.

Lynda Ashmore's Devon Rex Queen 'Cralahome Fabiol Tabby' (lovingly known at home as 'Flabby Tabby') is greedy to say the least, and like all smart little Rex cats she will stop at nothing to get to something she wants badly. In the light of 'Flabby Tabby's' greedy

Above: Devon Rex kittens are always up to some sort of mischief.
Left: Devon Rex – mother and child.
Below: A wide-eyed look from 'Tiger Lily'.

nature, Lynda made up her mind that the little cat's waistline had to be considered. Treats were dutifully placed on a high shelf over the cooker hood, well out of reach. Or so she thought!

Lynda lives in South Yorkshire, so as one might expect, she is a dab hand at batter pudding. One Sunday, the mixture, beautifully prepared was standing in a bowl on the kitchen work surface. 'Flabby Tabby' spotted her treats and jumped up onto the high shelf to reach them. She then proceeded to knock the contents of the packet down and straight into the basin of batter. Shock horror! A fresh start was the only option – Lynda rushed to the fridge to get more eggs. Unfortunately she discovered that she didn't have any. Sunday Roast without Yorkshire Pud? Unheard of! Quick thinking was required – quick thinking and a sieve. Lynda reasoned that as 'Flabby' hadn't actually come into contact with the treats, it would be alright to take them out again. The pudding was duly made and Lynda's husband Ian thoroughly enjoyed his Sunday roast, commenting at the time that the

pudding had an exceptionally tasty nutty flavour.

Lynda Ashmore and Anne West run the Devon Rex re-homing scheme. Lynda prefers the term re-homing rather than rescue, as sadly, the majority of cats which come her way are the victims of separation or divorce. She is always on the look out for permanent loving homes for these delightful little cats, so if anyone is interested in helping, please call Lynda or Anne on 01142 586866. These two ladies are the backbone of the scheme and they have worked together diligently as a team since the formation of the Rex Cat Association in 1989.

HAVANA

Eventually their beauty was recognised and the Havana Brown self-coloured Siamese cat was developed.

*L*ike the Oriental, the Havana cat is a 'Siamese' at heart. Brown pointed Siamese were popular in the 1930s and occasionally self-coloured brown kittens were born. It is possible that they appeared through the introduction of some brown Burmese bloodlines. This may well have happened by accident or as a deliberate experiment to strengthen the brown point colour of the Siamese cats. We will never know for certain, but apparently the self-coloured kittens were considered undesirable, with the breeders just retaining the 'pointed' cats. Some stories state that the self-coloured kittens were concealed, with many breeders almost denying their existence. However, a number survived, and eventually their beauty was recognised and the Havana Brown self-coloured Siamese cat was developed. Their beautiful apple green eyes probably stem from the introduction of even more brown or black Burmese bloodlines until eventually these lovely cats began to breed true to type. After a while other solid colours were developed as the popularity of these cats increased. This breakaway breed eventually became known as 'Oriental' and the cat which was originally called 'Havana Brown' because of its similarity to the colour of a Havana cigar, became the 'Oriental Chestnut' (we have featured an Oriental Cinnamon on page 69). With the continued development of the Oriental more colours were introduced, but the 'Oriental Chestnut' became more and more popular until this solid brown cat appeared in sufficient numbers to be recognised as a separate breed type. Then came another change of name, this time to just 'Havana'. I believe this occurred in 1991 and the breed has now gone on from strength to strength, so much so that at the GCCF Supreme Show at the NEC in November 1994, the overall winner was a Havana. This cat was Supreme Grand Champion and Grand Premier 'Rimana Sangria', owned by Christine and Brian Wooller of Cheshire. 'Sangria' was given to

Eye Colour – *Clear, bright vivid green with no flecks of contrasting colour.*

Coat Colour – *Rich warm chestnut brown. Not dark or cold toned.*

Nose Leather and Eye Rims – *Brown or pinkish brown.*

Paw Pads – *Solid brown or solid pinkish brown.*

Withhold Certificates for First Prizes in Kitten Open Classes for:

1. Colour not rich warm chestnut brown to the roots.
2. Scattered white hairs.
3. Rusty or other shadings in the coat.
4. General Oriental withholding faults.

the Woollers as a Christmas present from the good friends Marina and Michael Ward, well-known breeders of Orientals and Havanas.

The kitten was renamed 'Leon' which spelt backwards is, of course, 'Noel'. Now two years old, 'Leon' is an exquisite creature, solid brown with a coat of pure silk, his eyes a gorgeous green. 'Leon's' favourite pastime is knocking the phone off the hook and hitting the buttons with his paw until he hears a voice saying,

Ben Challenger with 'Django'.

'Your number has not been recognised please replace your receiver'. An obvious star, perhaps he thinks he is calling his agent. What next – Hollywood?

The cat in the main picture on the previous page is 'Cantabile Django'.

'Django', who is three years old, belongs to Ben Challenger who is at present the English Schools Under-17 High Jump Champion and is hoping for a Sports Scholarship to study athletics in the USA. 'Django' and Ben are inseparable and both live very active lives. Like Ben, 'Django' is an ace high jumper, he does brilliant backflips as he catches flies. So successful is he that

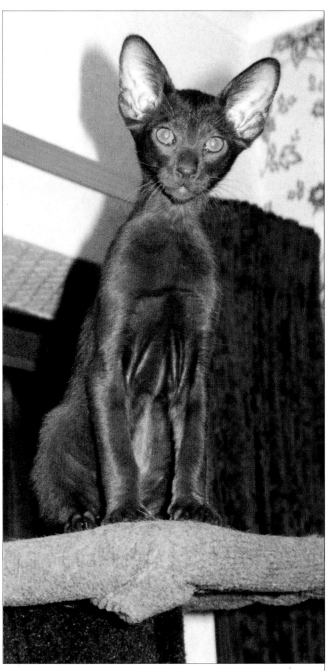

A high vantage point for 'Brandy' and (right) a coy look from the folds of a silk drape.

Ben's mother Dawn no longer bothers to buy fly spray! 'Django' is too smart for his own good. Dawn has already had to go to the expense of buying a brand new refrigerator as 'Django' was so adept at opening the old one that food disappeared at an alarming rate.

MAINE COON

The port of Maine was host to a large number of trader and clipper ships and almost every one had a cat.

There have been stories of the existence of large handsome long-haired bushy tailed cats in the State of Maine since the 1700s. Just exactly how they evolved remains a mystery, but they did *not* result from a chance mating between a wild cat and a racoon. Such a mating would be both physically and genetically impossible! Furthermore they bear no resemblance to racoons, which I can assure you are the most uncat-like creatures. They are delightful pointy faced clown-like creatures, dextrous with their 'hands', their little fingers long and human-like. They prefer to hold their food when eating and to wash each piece if water is available. I worked with several during my time in Hollywood, and know from experience that they are nothing like the Maine Coon cat.

We *do* know, however, that two hundred years ago the port of Maine was host to a large number of trader and clipper ships and almost every one had a cat. In those days a cat was an essential member of any ship's company, as it would earn its keep by controlling the ever-present vermin. When the vessels were docked and divested of their cargos, their crews would go ashore to find some rest and 'recreation' and the cats would doubtless have followed suit, seeking out their mates among the local feline community. As many ships came in from Scandinavia it is quite possible that some of these cats were related to the semi-long-haired bushy tailed felines from the Norwegian forests. There certainly is a striking resemblance.

My favourite story (although probably the least

The Maine Coon evolved as a working domesticated cat in a rural environment; this produced a muscular cat of rugged outdoor appearance with a character-istic weatherproof coat and the demeanour of an alert capable hunter.

Head *– Medium in length, the nasal bridge being equidistant from the ear line and the tip of the nose, with the width being slightly less than the length of the head. Allowance should be made for additional breadth or jowls in mature males. The muzzle should be square with a firm chin; chin, upper lip and nose leather should fall in a perpendicular line. Cheeks fairly full with high cheek bones. Bite level. Nose of uniform width with a shallow concave curve at the nasal bridge when viewed in profile and without a sharp break or stop.*

Ears *– Large, tall ears, wide at the base and tapering to appear pointed at the tip; set high but well apart.*

Eyes *– Full and round, spaced wide apart with a slightly oblique aperture and set. Shades of green, gold or copper; coat and eye colour may be unrelated. Odd or blue eyes are permissible in white cats.*

Body and Neck *– Large to medium size, solid and muscular with breadth of chest. Long back with proportionate limbs to create the characteristic rectangular appearance; square rump. Neck moderately long; particularly thick and muscular in mature males.*

Legs and Paws *– Substantial legs with large round paws; toes carried close, five in front, four behind.*

Tail *– Long, at least the length of the back, wide at the base and tapering towards the tip.*

Coat *– Waterproof and virtually self-maintaining, consisting of an undercoat covered by a more substantial glossy top coat. Fur shorter on the head, neck*

and shoulders increasing in length down the back, flanks and tail. A fluffy appearance is undesirable. Breeches and belly fur full and shaggy. Frontal ruff beginning at the base of the ears; heavier in males than females. Tail fur long, profuse and flowing; not bushy. Ears feathered and preferably tufted at the tips; the ear feathering should extend beyond the outer edges of the ear. Paws tufted, with long tufts emanating from under the paws extending backwards to create snowshoe effect.

likely) is the tale of Captain Clough, a New England seadog who was hard-headed and had a strong reputation for business. In the late 1700s the French aristocracy was in a perilous situation, none more so than Queen Marie Antoinette herself. There was no doubt that she felt her security was in jeopardy and that her days of luxurious living could well be numbered. With this thought in mind she apparently arranged for a large consignment of her personal effects

have felt that she couldn't start life in a new land without at least a few of her treasured pets. Whatever the truth of this story, these cats were apparently set free to mix and mate with the locals. Wouldn't it be nice to think that all Maine Coons carry a small drop of French aristocratic blue blood in their veins?

Maine Coon cats have been breeding true to type for at least 200 years. They are large, sturdy, handsome creatures with lion-like ruffs around their necks and

Above: Amanda and David Thomas with arms full of pretty Maine Coon kittens.
Above right: A fold of little Maine Coons.

to be shipped to the port of Maine, under the care of Captain Clough, who would doubtless have been offered a large reward, considering the risk he took placing both himself and his crew in extreme danger.

The story goes that the French Queen was to have followed shortly after the despatch of her belongings, but as we all know from our history books, this was not to be! However, her goods and chattels eventually arrived in Maine and Captain Clough kept his promise and arranged for safe storage. In due course the news of Marie Antoinette's sad demise reached the American shores and her goods were eventually disposed of, possibly to offset the unpaid bill. Included in her household effects were six longhaired cats. The Queen was known to be a lover of small animals and may well

thick fluffy 'breeches' on their back legs. They are easy-going and affectionate with hardly any hereditary defects, and have nice, straight, easy breathing noses and long strong bones. Their ears are tipped with distinctive tufts.

Their tails are fantastic, forming thick plume-like brushes which wrap majestically around their front

A long stretch for 'Meddy', who measures 42 inches from paw to paw!

'Fuzzy' – a six-week-old red-shaded Maine Coon kitten.

paws when they sit. They are delightful cats to live with and even though they do require some grooming, they are well worth the effort. If you would like a big cat with personality and presence, then this is certainly one to consider.

The Maine Coon Breed Society has been in existence in the USA for over 25 years while the United Kingdom Maine Coon Cat Club was formed in the late 1980s. The showing of Maine Coons in the United Kingdom has grown in popularity over the past ten years, so much so that the Governing Council granted the breed Championship Status in 1993, with the classes getting steadily larger. It seems more and more Coon owners are trying their luck and having fun days out at the shows. Win or lose, who cares? Even the cats seem to enjoy it.

The cat in the main picture on page 49 is 'Amoracoon Tundra'.

Amanda Thomas of South West London, with support from her husband David, has been breeding Maine Coons since 1988 when she bought her first, a red tabby girl 'Rosamund', and became enchanted with the cats. Amanda, who never does anything by halves, made a point of studying the breed and she has been producing kittens with steady improvement ever since. Both Amanda and David have become extremely knowledgeable, and Amanda is now the Overseas Director of the Maine Coon Breed Fanciers Association, the American Society of Maine Coons. For the last two years Amanda has been researching into Feline Genetics at the University of London. She has published a book, *Genetics for the Maine Coon Cat Breeder*, which is a must for any novice owner considering breeding for the first time.

'Tundra', named for obvious reasons, is an odd-eyed white. This is not a fault but a breed colour recognised by the Governing Council. 'Tundra' is two years old and a bundle of fun. He was super to photograph and rose to the occasion, taking no notice whatsoever of the lights, umbrellas and paraphernalia which Geoff and his assistant Simon set up around him. When asked to sit on the set on a small plinth behind the roll of rope, he behaved like an old hand; not once did he try to jump down, preferring to stay and take in the ambience. My kind of cat! This is the temperament I search for when I need an animal to photograph. 'Tundra' is a trouper and one I shall remember for the future should I require a long-haired white for a photo

Charlotte and 'Tundra'.

shoot. Amanda tells me that 'Tundra' has always been the same and it was his temperament which made her decide not to sell him in the first place. She has a small daughter, Charlotte, and as a kitten 'Tundra' was amazingly tolerant of the little girl, and the two became inseparable. Charlotte and 'Tundra' are still a pair, and always seem to be together somewhere in the house. But he has not always been 'whiter than white' – there have been several times when he has blotted his copy book. Until Amanda blocked off her fireplace with a solid guard, 'Tundra' had the habit of climbing up the chimney (when the fire was out, of course) and emerging to qualify for a rename as 'Sooty' and spreading the evidence all over the carpets and furniture. No one is purrfect.

MANX

AND THEREBY HANGS A TAIL (OR NOT)

There have been tailless or partially tailed cats on the Isle of Man for at least 200 years.

Most people think of Manx cats as completely tailless and coming from the Isle of Man. Well, this is partly true – they *did* originate on the island, but many pure bred Manx do have tails (or at least tails of sorts). The completely tailless cat is known as a 'Rumpy': it is nicely rounded at the back end, with a slight hollow at the base of the spine where the tail would be. This is the perfect Manx.

Then there are 'Rumpy Risers'. These are *almost* tailless, but do have a small amount of bone or gristle at the end of the spine, which can easily be felt, even if not evident to the eye. These are the only two types which may be shown to achieve Championship status in the United Kingdom.

A pure bred Manx cat may produce tails of varying lengths in any one litter, from the 'Rumpy' type to fully tailed kittens. This will not mean that the mother cat has had a dalliance with a non-pedigree boy; indeed it seems that two pure bred 'Rumpies' frequently produce litters of varying tail lengths.

How did these cats evolve? No one really knows for sure. As with many breeds, attractive but dubious legends purport to explain their origins. In 1588, many ships of the defeated Spanish Armada were wrecked in terrible storms on their desperate flight back to Spain. One came to grief on the rocks near Spanish Point on the Isle of Man; a handful of intrepid cats survived the waters and landed on the island, founding the race of Manx cats. It's a tale that appeals to the imagination, but has no basis in fact: if it were true, wouldn't Spain have its own line of tailless cats too? Another story maintains that merchant ships of the sixteenth century brought the first Manx cats from the Far East, and tantalisingly, tailless cats *do* exist in Japan. But as in so many cases the feline historian is thwarted by the lack of accurate records before the Victorian era.

There have been tailless or partly tailed cats on the Isle of Man for at least 200 years, mostly in rural areas. The tailless cat may well have evolved from a mutation and as felines will interbreed if left to their own devices, a small colony probably developed on the island. They are sturdy, farm-type cats who have, over generations, developed an amazing coat. At first glance the Manx just looks like any other close-coated puss, and it is only when one actually handles them that one discovers the amazingly thick weather-proof undercoat,

---

Head – *Fairly round and large with prominent cheeks. Nose broad and straight, of medium length without break. Strong muzzle without any hint of snipiness. Firm chin and even bite.*

Ears – *Fairly tall, set rather high on the head and angled slightly outwards. Open at base tapering to a narrow, rounded tip.*

Eyes – *Large and round. Colour preferably in keeping with coat colour.*

Body – *Solid, compact, with good breadth of chest and short back ending in a definite round rump. The rump to be higher than the shoulder.*

Flanks of great depth.

Legs – *Of good substance with front legs short and well set to show good breadth of chest. Back legs longer than the front with powerful, deep thighs.*

Taillessness – *Absolute taillessness is essential. The rump should be left to be completely rounded with no definite rise of bone or cartilage interfering with the roundness of the rump.*

Coat – *Double-coated showing a well padded quality arising from a short, very thick undercoat and a slightly longer overcoat. The double quality of the coat is of far more importance than*

colour or markings, which should be taken into account only if all other points are equal.

Colours and Patterns – *All colours and patterns are acceptable with the exception of the 'Siamese' pattern.*

almost cushion-like, lying below the outer hair. This makes these cats tough and capable of tolerating extreme weather conditions. Indeed, one breeder friend of mine tells me that her most difficult task is trying to shampoo her Manx for show. It seems that the water from her hand shower just runs straight off, leaving the skin bone dry. In an effort to preserve the true characteristics of the breed, this weather-proof coat is now prized by show people.

It is not unknown for the occasional long-haired Manx kitten to be born but these may not be shown in the United Kingdom as they do not appear in sufficient numbers. They have, however, been bred and shown in the USA and in Europe, and they are known as 'Cymric' cats – Cymric meaning Celtic.

A Manx is a great indoor and outdoor pet, and with the exception of basic vaccinations, should cost very

Left: Alina Beresford with 'Nyna'.
Below: 'Tatleberry Tudur' and friend go hunting.

little in vets bills. They are long-lived and sturdy, and will give companionship and affection in abundance. This breed may not be uppermost in the mind when one is considering buying a pure bred cat for the first time, but they really do have so much to offer. What of the Manx temperament? They have solid easygoing natures and must be one of the most underrated of the pure breeds. They are well worth considering, and if one is fortunate enough to obtain a true 'Rumpy', what a conversation piece one has! Kittens are not plentiful, but may occasionally be obtained from one of a very small group of dedicated breeders.

The cat in the main picture on the page 53 is 'Grand Champion Chatterly Mianyn' – 'Nyna'.

'Nyna' is a true 'Rumpy', classified as a Torti and White Tabby, bred by her owner Alina Beresford from West Yorkshire. These cats make outstandingly good parents, the queens dote on their kittens, giving them constant attention. 'Nyna' is no exception. She recently produced three lovely babies (two like herself, torti and white and one with red tabby markings) which she cared for in a basket by the kitchen stove. Another of Alina's cats, 'Minnie', also had a litter of similar age,

and her three pure cream kittens were safely tucked up with their mother in another part of the house. One Saturday morning Alina checked the mother cats to see that all was well and then popped out to do some shopping. Upon her return to the kitchen, she glanced into 'Nyna's' basket and was amazed to discover that the babies had miraculously changed colour! Three *cream* kittens were being scrubbed and fed, a perfect picture of contentment; in the other room 'Minnie' was busying herself with two torti and white kittens and one red tabby. The Manx are such superb mothers that their strong maternal instincts reach far and beyond their own offspring. Apparently it is not unusual for them to form a communal crèche with two queens sharing the maternal duties, tending to and feeding both litters. Perhaps this behaviour stems back to when the cats lived in colonies many generations ago, when unity would have meant strength.

Left: 'Where's my tail?' 'Molley' seems surprised to find nothing there.
Above: 'Minnie', an elegant blue, torti and white, poses on the table.

MIXED BREEDS

It was the Egyptians who brought the cat into our lives.

As we've seen, many breeds well known today were first imported to the West within the last 150 years, and many others have been deliberately created within living memory. But cats have been in Britain for centuries: what were they like before the rise of pedigrees and the precise classifications set in motion by enthusiastic late Victorians?

There were small wildcats over most of the UK thousands of years ago. But millennia of cultivation and the clearing of ancient forests – and above all, the unstoppable spread of mankind – have made them very rare indeed. The European wildcat (*Felis silvestris silvestris*), a variable, mainly tabby creature, still survives in small populations in Scotland: some experts even want to make it a distinct subspecies (named *Felis silvestris grampia*) because of differences in the colour of its coat. Though they will interbreed with domestic cats, these nervous inhabitants of Scotland's heathlands aren't the ancestors of our many millions of moggies!

That honour almost certainly goes to another subspecies – the African wildcat (*Felis silvestris lybica*). It's another tabby cat whose coat ranges from a pale yellowish grey to quite dark steely colours. Compared to its descendants it is noticeably heftier, quite chunky in fact. In nature this handsome predator is found mainly in woodlands or the vast open grasslands that so characterise wild Africa.

When did cats become domesticated? Certainly a long time ago. Most theories maintain that the ancient Egyptians brought the cat into our lives. There's plenty of evidence for cats in their civilisation from about 1500 BC onwards. Piecing together the next stage in the early history of the cat is a task frustrated by gaps in what few records there are, but once more art gives us some clues. Starting around 500 BC cats are shown on painted pottery and carved stone reliefs from Ancient Greece. What's more, the bones of cats are increasingly found on archaeological sites of this period. Then, in later centuries, as the Roman Empire rose to prominence, the cat was there too.

And it was the Romans who left us evidence of cats in the UK. Colchester in Essex was a major capital even before the Romans captured it; they soon made it one of the great centres of Roman Britain. A charming gravestone from the first or second century AD shows a child clutching a cat to its chest. From Colchester too come tiles with pawprints on them – some cat obviously ran across them before they had set; similar tiles have also been found at the Hampshire site of Silchester.

So we know there were cats then – but what did they look like? Mosaics from Rome show striped tabbies catching birds, but I haven't come across a similar one from Britain. Nonetheless tabbies of many kinds must have been prevalent. After the collapse of the Roman Empire, records and works of art are scarcer; pieces of legislation survive showing the valuable work cats did in keeping down vermin, but not surprisingly they don't talk about the appearance of these creatures. Great manuscripts from around 800 AD depict stylised cats in illuminated capital letters and on ornate borders to their pages. But while these designs capture essential feline facial features they rarely make it possible to see what these cats actually looked like.

Jumping forward to the early Middle Ages, we can see convincingly realistic cats in a number of books called bestiaries. They were religious works which used both animals from the real world and fictional fabulous creatures to tell parables. They show unmistakable short-haired cats, silvery tabbies, darker ones and pale-coloured cats, doing believable feline things – washing, catching rodents and so on. I haven't seen one that shows any kind of long hair.

After the Middle Ages cats appear in portrait paintings throughout Europe. In France longhairs were the playthings of the wealthy from the late sixteenth century onwards; but charming images of shorthairs adorn many paintings of children. Perhaps one of the finest is William Hogarth's *The Graham Children* from the eighteenth century – it's in the Tate Gallery, London. In it, a cheeky striped tabby peers covetously at a songbird in a cage from behind the top of an armchair.

A century later of course takes us into the Victorian age, that time of scientific advancement in all fields and a period of careful classification of the natural world – and the establishing of the breeds that so beautifully adorn this book.

MARVELLOUS MOGGIES

Cat behaviour is fascinating and I never cease to marvel at the intelligence of these creatures.

So much for the history of the mixed breed called variously the domestic short (or long) hair, non-pedigree, household pet or moggie, a cat formed by nature without any help from man. These cats are usually a great deal tougher than their pedigree cousins. Like the mongrel dog, the cat with mixed breeding should have hybrid vigour and with care will probably live to a ripe old age with very few problems. Vets bills should be low and visits to the surgery only necessary for annual vaccinations, spaying and neutering, dental checks and the like. But however lowly their origins, these cats will require the same care and attention as pure-bred pets and any prospective owner should bear these costs in mind. I have a number of moggies and I love them. They are all very individual with their own little characteristics. Some are very clever and I have cashed in on their natural talents. 'Mowgli', for example, discovered that he could open the door by the handle! Being a professional trainer, I encouraged this behaviour and started to 'pay' him with treats whenever he let himself in. The boot was soon on the other foot and he had me well and truly trained! After a while we had to keep the doors locked to prevent him from holding 'open house' for his friends! Cat behaviour is fascinating and I never cease to marvel at the intelligence of these creatures. Most of my working cats are of mixed breeding, rescued like 'Arthur' from unhappy circumstances. Our 'Stanley' for example was found when no more than a few weeks old, in a cardboard box, together with the rest of his litter, and handed in

'Mowgli' does his party piece.

to the Wood Green Animal Shelter. He is nine years old now, a super family pet and very territorial – he allows only his friends to visit and woe betide any strange cat who might stray into his garden!

I won't dwell too long on the training of cats, but it is quite possible if one understands the feline mentality and allows the animal to believe that it is in total control of the situation. One of my routines involves the cat sitting at a keyboard and depressing the keys for reward. I have five cats who will do this and over the years it has proved to be extremely useful.

Above: 'Sparkie', the cat with the hint of a squint.
Left: 'Pippin' sits patiently as six-month-old 'William Junior' practises his jumping technique.

'Sophie' has been filmed 'working' a computer; 'Jaffa', 'Sparkie' and 'Mowgli' have all been filmed playing their Yamaha. Now, I know that they are laughing at me when they perform. They really think that I am so daft that all they have to do is plonk on the keys with their paws and I will pay them! They use this trained behaviour to *demand* treats, so everyone is pleased.

'Jaffa' is the cat in the main picture on page 59 and another of my moggies 'Bertie' is featured in the main picture on page 57.

As the moggie cat carries traits from many of the pure breeds, it is fun to try to ascertain just which. The long hairs doubtless carry Persian blood, and because of their outcrossing they will probably have much more 'get up and go', and have open faces with straight 'easy breathing' noses. But if you are considering acquiring a fluffy crossbreed, don't be fooled into thinking that it won't require the same care and attention as a Persian. *All* long-haired cats must be groomed to prevent matts and tangles forming in the coat, which if left will eventually create lumps like felt; these may have to be cut away leaving bare patches, which may become infested or infected. Please don't let this put you off owning a fluffy cat – five or ten minutes every day is all it takes to keep your pet's coat in tip-top shape.

Our 'Sophie', a semi-long-haired mixed breed, is a super little girl with an amazing temperament. She is small, probably due to her poor start in life. I rescued two kittens from an appalling home, after seeing a post card in a shop window. The house was filthy, children were mishandling the kittens, carrying them by their legs and teasing them, and the litter tray under the table was full to the brim. I just grabbed both kitties (having gone there only for one) handed over my money and got out as quickly as I could. I re-homed the second kitten with a friend and started to rehabilitate mine, who soon developed into a little beauty. She is petite and doll-like, ultra feminine and a true pro! She has filmed countless commercials and has also made documentaries, appeared in TV dramas and played the part of 'Myrtle', the *Story Time* cat in the BBC children's series of the same name. She has gone from strength to strength and even

A perfect picture – 'Sophie' relaxes in an apple tree.

Above: 'Oliver' in his television role as 'Harry' in the 'Elmlea' commercial.
Right: Who needs a pedigree? 'William' proves that handsome is as handsome does.

now, at nine years of age, still looks and acts like an overgrown kitten.

Look at her closely and then turn to page 89. See the resemblance to the Turkish Van? Sophie has many of the Van traits, including her tolerance of water. Although I have never asked her to swim, she was once required to fish in a garden pond whilst filming for the *Ruth Rendell Mysteries*. This she did with ease, and she has never objected to taking a bath.

The background of the shorthaired moggie is sometimes a bit harder to work out. Our young 'Sparkie' may have a touch of Siamese. He is fine boned, has a hint of a squint and is very vocal. 'Oliver' on the other hand is long and lean, and in his heyday was very athletic, playing a leaping cat in pet food commercials of the 1980s. He is more sedate now but still has the look of a wild cat, a true hunter – Abyssinian perhaps? Who knows?

NORWEGIAN FOREST CAT

Norwegians maintain that these cats have been around for ever.

*L*egend has it that the Viking longboats carried cats to control vermin. These animals were of powerful build, strong, robust and very handsome, with semi-long silky top hair covering a thick weatherproof undercoat. Their tails were bushy and their long backlegs and powerful hindquarters rendered them fast and agile. They were great hunters and no doubt prized by their Viking masters. It's certainly believable that Vikings imported cats with the gene producing long hair from the Levant and the Middle East before the year 1000 – Viking traders travelled remarkable distances and were known to visit Constantinople (modern Istanbul) long before the Crusaders of the Middle Ages.

Norwegians maintain that these cats (the *Norsk Skaukatt* as they say) have been around forever. For centuries they roamed wild in the forest areas of Scandinavia, where they lived on small rodents and birds, and have been known to fish. But sadly, by the 1930s, their numbers had started to decline. Fortunately their outgoing disposition made them easy to capture, and by the late 1960s a group of dedicated breeders in Norway had made an all-out effort to save the cats from extinction and a breeding programme was well under way by the mid 1970s. By then, they had produced enough stock of suitable quality to apply to have the breed accepted by the European governing body for championship status. Now they are prized and shown all over Europe and the USA. So far they have remained scrupulously true to type, totally unspoiled as nature intended.

At the time of writing (July 1995) Norwegian Forest cats do not qualify for championship status in the UK. However, the breed is already well up to provisional standard, and hopefully within two years, these beautiful creatures will have acquired full GCCF recognition, and will be able to compete at the top level. In side classes it is not unknown for Norwegian Forest cats to win over full champions from other semi-long haired breeds.

Anyone owning a Norwegian Forest cat must be prepared to spend time with it. The breed is gregarious and loves company. The cats require toys to keep them amused as they are very intelligent. Being natural hunters, and having used their wits to survive in the wild, they need lots of mental and physical stimuli. A second cat is a good idea as the pair will play and mock hunt together, but you must supply some sort of climbing equipment, and a scratching post if you value your furniture and curtains. They will live happily in an apartment but adore a garden.

Norwegian Forest cats will climb to the highest tip

Head – *Triangular, long straight profile without break in line. Strong chin.*

Ears – *High and open, with good width at the base (width between ears being less than the width of one ear), high set so that the lines of the ears follow the line of the head down to the chin. With lynx-like tufts and long hair out of the ears.*

Eyes – *Large, well-opened, slightly oblique. All colours allowed, regardless of coat colour.*

Body and Legs – *Big and strongly built, high on the legs, the hind legs higher than the front ones. Solid bone structure.*

Tail – *Long and bushy, should reach at least to the shoulder blades.*

Coat – *Semi-long. The woolly undercoat is covered by a smooth water-repellent overcoat. This glossy hair covers the back and the sides. A fully coated cat has a shirt-front, a full ruff and knickerbockers.*

(During summer months the coat is considerably shorter).

Above: Pat and Neil Stewart with 'Alfie'.

The cat in the main picture on the previous page is 'Skogens Aldsveder' – 'Alfie'.

'Alfie' is a first generation English-bred cat from imported parents and lives with his half-brother 'Tigger' ('Skogens Sigi') and his breeder/owners Pat and Neil Stewart in Berkshire. (Aldsveder was one of the two horses that pulled the Chariot of the Moon in Norse Mythology.)

Pat and Neil bought their first Norwegian Forest cat in 1993, when their two grown sons moved out to start their own homes and they were left with just one elderly moggie, 'Sam'. Sadly, only a few days later, the old boy died; the house was suddenly empty. Pat and Neil set out to replace 'Sam' with another similar cat. They tried various places to no avail, there were no crossbred kittens to be had anywhere. They hadn't even thought of a pure breed until they saw an advertisement in the paper for new Norwegian Forest kittens. What had they got to lose?

They went, they saw, and they came away with 'Tigger', a bouncy, friendly six-months-old neutered boy. Pat and Neil felt from the start that here was something completely different from any cat they had ever known before. They were enchanted. The loveable little character soon filled the house with fun

of the tallest tree, and then scamper down again head first, clinging like limpets with their wide feet and long claws, tails flying out behind. This is a sight not to be missed. They have often been described in fun as a cross between a small dog and a squirrel. They require little grooming in the winter, but in the spring they will shed their entire undercoat in a matter of days, so have your brush and comb handy as the temperature rises.

Above: Red and tabby Norwegian Forest kittens share a bed with two blue Abyssinians.
Below and below left: 'Volsung Dustin' with her seven-week-old daughter 'Eviva'.

and it wasn't long before they bought a second kitten for company.

Now Pat and Neil have a completely new interest. They are keen members of the Norwegian Forest Cat Club and find attending shows great fun – it's a chance to meet and talk with other NFC owners, and win or lose, have a good day out. That's what cat showing is all about! They are now the proud owners of four NFCs and they are looking forward to breeding their first litter with 'Alfie' as the proud dad.

'Alfie' is two-year-old with a typical NFC temperament, cheerful and lively. A bit of a chatterbox, he is very sociable and loves attention. When he is in a happy mood he 'chirrups', particularly when dinner time approaches. 'Alfie' is already doing well in the show ring and was the Norwegian Forest Cat Club Best Tabby of the Year in 1994. A Champ in the making?

ORIENTAL SHORTHAIR

They are chatterboxes, attention seekers and intelligent.

To this day self-coloured or solid Siamese cats occur occasionally in Thailand (formerly Siam) as they probably did hundreds of years ago. It is quite possible that when the first plain brown Siamese cats (now known as Havanas), first appeared in England in the 1930s, they were throwbacks from their ancient ancestors. These beautiful animals received help along the way from breeders who could see that they were well worth developing as a separate breed. Like the Havana, the Oriental is a Siamese cat without the 'points', sleek and svelte, elegant and slender, with wedge shaped heads and widely spaced ears. All varieties of Oriental share Siamese cats' personality traits. They are chatterboxes, attention seekers, possess intelligence and are almost dog-like. They love exercise and will play for hours. Devoted to their owners, they demand to be spoiled and praised. These days the Oriental now appears in a variety of gorgeous colours, each distinct shade now known as a separate breed; 'Oriental Black', 'Oriental White', and so on. The Siamese is famous for its sapphire blue eyes but several different eye colours appear in the Oriental cats. The Oriental Cinnamon opposite has green eyes.

The cat in the main picture is 'Petrajeen Lionheart Simba'.

'Simba' is a seven-month-old kitten, the pride and joy of Maureen and Roy Fall of Warwickshire. Named after the cub in the Disney film *The Lion King,* 'Simba' is a bundle of mischief, darting like quicksilver from one prank to the next. Naturally curious, he was fascinated with the lights and paraphernalia which Geoff and Simon had arranged for his photo session, and he took a particular shine to the Lasto-Light reflector. He genuinely thought that the whole set up had been put there solely for his amusement! But as one can see from the picture, he did eventually pose beautifully for us.

He didn't actually 'say' a great deal during the shoot, but according to Maureen he can 'talk' the hind leg off a donkey, and apparently when he is taken to the vet his protest can be heard two blocks away. At home,

---

The Oriental should be a beautifully balanced animal with head and ears carried on a slender neck and with a long svelte body supported on fine legs and feet, with a slender, whipped tail, free from abnormalities. The body, legs, feet, head and tail should all be in proportion, giving a well balanced appearance. The expression should be alert and intelligent. The cat should be in excellent physical condition.

Head and Neck – Head long and well proportioned with width between the ears and narrowing in perfectly straight lines to a fine muzzle and forming a balanced triangle with no break or pinch at the whiskers. The head and profile should be wedge-shaped, neither round nor pointed, avoiding exaggerated type. In profile the nose should be straight, free from any stop or dip, and the chin should be strong with a level bite. The tip of the chin should line up with the tip of the nose in the same vertical plane. The neck should be long and slender.

Ears – Large, pricked and wide at the base with their setting continuing the lines of the wedge.

Eyes – Oriental in shape and slanting towards the nose with good width between. No tendency to squint.

Body – Medium in size. Long and svelte with a tight abdomen, firm and well-muscled throughout.

Legs and Paws – Legs long and slim. Hind legs higher than the front legs.

Legs to be firm and well muscled. Paws small and oval.

Tail – Long and tapering. Not blunt ended, and free from any abnormality of the bone structure.

Coat – Very short and fine in texture. Glossy and close-lying. Even and sound throughout in adults and free from any flakes of dead skin.

Above: An Oriental tabby copies his cartoon hero 'Top Cat' and takes to the dustbin.
Right: Maureen Fall with 'Simba'.

'Simba' is an avid snooker fan and will watch the TV with fascination as the balls go whizzing across the screen. Every so often, his curiosity will get the better of him and he will peep behind the set just to see if anything has dropped out at the back! 'Simba' is also keen on *Gardeners' World*, and Maureen has stopped buying fresh cut flowers as he takes a great delight in doing his own bit of horticultural re-arranging. 'Simba' shares his home with other cats, but as the baby of the family he tends to create havoc and let the others take the blame. He has a habit of shutting himself into cupboards and then crying to be let out again and Maureen has to follow the plaintive sounds around the house until she finds him.

But 'Simba' does have his good points! Meticulously clean and easy to live with, he is not in the least destructive and he has never swung on the curtains or sharpened his nails anywhere except on his scratching post. A gentleman in the making?

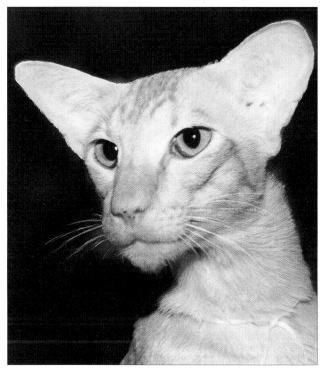

Below: Two Oriental tabbies pose for the camera with three Havana kittens.
Above: Two handsome fellows, Oriental red 'Warhed Azeem' and (right) Oriental black and Supreme UK Grand Premier 'Warhed Rashed'.

RAGDOLL

ZZZZZZ...

They are so laid back that they are said to go limp when picked up.

Home loving, quiet, retiring and tranquil. All of these descriptions have been attributed to the 'Rag Doll Cat' since it first appeared in the USA in the 1950s. The breed may well have developed from Birmans, as the 'Rag Doll' does show a marked similarity to the Birman Cat (another very easygoing gentle breed); one variety of 'Rag Doll' even wears the white Birman mittens. It is possible that Siamese, Colour Points and Persians might be in the mix, too.

The 'Rag Doll Cat' cannot claim exotic myths and legends in its ancestry. What happened was this. Kittens of an amazing, almost unnaturally placid nature were born in California to a white Persian queen who had mis-mated with an unknown male. One story says that the mother cat had been involved in a car accident prior to the birth, and that she had suffered a fractured pelvis; the kittens were tranquil as a result of surviving this accident. Of course, this cannot possibly be true as the physical injuries of the mother could not have had any effect on the characteristics of the offspring. However, for whatever reason, these kittens were of an exceptionally gentle and placid disposition. They were so extraordinary that when bred from, the temperament carried through to the next generation. Breeders were so intrigued by these kittens that more litters were produced and gradually the numbers increased. The name 'Rag Doll' is very apt as these cats are so laid back that they are said to go limp when picked up! Napoleon's famous adage 'Never stand when you can sit and never sit when you can lie' fits these cats to a tee. 'Rag Doll' cats were recognised as a breed in the USA in the 1960s and were brought over to the UK in the late 1970s or early 1980s.

When they arrived in England the cats created a

Head – Skull medium to large size, flat plane between ears. Cheeks well developed, tapering to a rounded well developed muzzle and firm chin with a level bite. The nose should have a very gentle break and be of medium length.

Ears – Medium in size, broad at the base with a slight tilt forward. Medium furnishings (tufts) in the ears. The ears should be rounded at the tip, set wide on the skull.

Eyes – Large, oval, set with a slight slant. Outer edge of the eye aperture to be level with the base of the ear. Blue in colour; the deeper blue the better.

Body and Neck – The body is long and muscular. The neck should be short, strong and heavy set. Chest should be broad and well expanded. Full maturity is achieved between three and four years of age.

Legs and Paws – Legs must be medium in length and of medium heavy bone. Hind legs to be slightly higher than the front. The paws should be large, round, firm and tufted.

Tail – The tail should be long, bushy, slightly tapered towards the tip and in proportion to the body.

Coat – Silky texture, dense, medium length, lying with the body and parting as the cat moves. Short on the face. Longer around the neck framing the face. Short over the shoulders. Medium length on the back, sides, abdomen and hindquarters. Short to medium length on the front legs. (Seasonal variations in coat shall be recognised.)

Colours – Good contrast is required between the points and body colour. Lack of contrast is considered a fault. Allowances should be made for incomplete masks and maturity of colour in kittens and younger cats (under 3 years). Mature cats with lighter back colouring are preferred. Ragdolls come in a variety of colours.

great deal of interest due to the mystery of their background. Now the 'Rag Doll Cat' is well received by the cat fancy and is gaining popularity every year. 'Rag Dolls' much prefer to lounge around at home than to go out on the prowl. Never ones to go in search of trouble, they are reputed to be stoical and non-aggressive and will not retaliate if challenged. As for their looks, they are handsome gentle giants with deep

a variety of attractive colours. The 'Rag Doll' is ideal for someone who wants a pet to supply love and companionship in abundance, a peaceful cat to complement a simple lifestyle.

The cat in the main picture on the previous page is 'Benachitti Phantomiser' – 'Phantom'.

'Phantom' is one of six 'Rag Doll' cats owned by Madeleine and Gordon Whittaker from the West Midlands. A perfect example of 'Phantom's' temperament is the true story of the wedding hat. Maureen had been invited to a wedding, and she had bought a new fur-trimmed hat (fake fur, of course) for the occasion. A day or so before the big event a friend dropped in for coffee. The two chatted about the forthcoming nuptials and the friend (as girls do) asked if she could try on the new hat. 'It's on the table in the dining room,' said Maureen. 'Help yourself.' The friend disappeared into the next room and a moment later a squeal was heard, and 'Oh my God, it's alive'. It seems that the hat *had* been on the table, but it had fallen down onto the floor; however, 'Phantom' was curled up in a tight ball fast asleep in the exact spot where the hat had been. It was only after the lady had actually picked him up (still curled) and tried to raise him to her head, that he moved. He yawned and stretched, and after she had put him down, promptly nodded off again. This could only happen with a 'Rag Doll' cat.

Madeleine and Gordon Whittaker with 'Phantom' and two 'babydolls'.

sapphire blue eyes and attractive 'Birman Points'. Their coats are long and silky and will require some grooming, their tails are thick and bushy. As a result of careful selective breeding these cats now appear in

Maureen told me that these cats are easy to train and will do as they are told. I believe this, as 'Phantom' behaved beautifully on the day we took his photograph, flicking his tail and showing himself off to perfection. He got the hang of posing very quickly. It was almost as if he were thinking to himself, 'Let's get this over with as quickly as possible, it's past my siesta time!'

Right: At home with 'Moon' and 'Dusty'.

Below: Adventure time for two other Ragdoll kittens.

RUSSIAN BLUE

Look into the eyes of a Russian Blue and you will see two of the most exquisite jewels.

Hear our prayer, Lord, for all animals. May they be well fed and well treated and happy. Protect them from hunger and fear and suffering: and we pray, protect especially dear Lord the little blue cat who is the companion of our home. Keep her safe as she goes abroad and bring her back to comfort us.

In ancient Russia it was considered customary for fairies to bestow gifts upon newborn royal babies, to ensure a long happy and fruitful life. On one such occasion an infant princess lay crying in her cradle. A group of fairies entered her room: the first carried a fearless spirit, the second a loyal heart. The third brought exquisite beauty and the fourth, grace and elegance. The fifth brought a promise that the royal infant should always be clad in silk and velvet, the sixth held a satin-lined casket containing two brilliant emeralds and the seventh brought a promise that the baby princess should be much loved and find many friends. As the fairies crossed the room the baby's cries became louder, so loud that the cradle rocked and the infant's face turned red. The fairies could not imagine how this squalling little brat could ever grow up to be a beautiful princess worthy of their gifts so instead they laid them in a small basket situated at the foot of the cradle. Sleeping in the basket was a beautiful blue cat – a gentle purring creature who was a much more fitting recipient.

When one meets a pure bred Russian Blue for the first time it is easy to see that those legendary gifts have been carried through the generations. These cats *do* have a fine and fearless spirit and most definitely loyal hearts. They adore their owners, and make fine companions and as for beauty and grace, they are almost matchless! They have fine muscular bodies and a supple flowing movement, and just as the fifth fairy promised all those years ago, their lush close coats feel like velvet and shine like pure silk. As for the casket containing two emeralds, look into the eyes of a Russian Blue and you will see two of the most exquisite jewels. Who could not help but love these creatures? As the seventh fairy promised, they charm everyone they meet.

Head – Short wedge with flat appearance between ears. In profile forehead and nose should appear straight, meeting at an angle level with the upper edge of the eye; there should be no stop or break. Prominent whisker pads. Strong chin with level bite. The tip of the chin should line up with the tip of the nose in the same vertical plane.

Ears – Large and pointed, wide at base with little inside hair and set vertically to the head.

Eyes – Vivid green, except in the case of the kittens where allowance should be made for eye colour. Set rather wide apart, almond in shape.

Body – Long and graceful in outline and carriage. Medium strong bone. Cobby or heavy build undesirable.

Legs and Feet – Long legs, feet small and oval.

Tail – Moderately long and tapering in proportion to the body. Neither blunt-ended nor whip. The tail should be free from any abnormality of bone structure.

Coat – The texture of the coat and appearance of the coat are the truest criteria of the Russian. The coat is double, short, thick and very fine, standing up soft and silky, very different in texture from any other breed.

They generate their own affection with their sweet gentle easygoing natures.

Blue cats similar to the pure breed of today have long been highly valued in Russia. The threads of the legend have been handed down through generations and many Russian peasants still believe that if one of these cats is placed in a basket at the foot of an infant's cradle, it will generate good fortune. The origins of these cats are lost in distant time. Some say that the Viking ships carried them; it is also possible that Russian traders kept them on their boats. Eventually they found their way to England via the port of Archangel in Northern Russia, hence the name 'Archangel Cat'. The first Russian cat to be shown in this country was reputed to have arrived on a boat, with Russian sailors exchanging it for a leg of lamb! There is a tradition that Queen Victoria and Prince Albert owned Russian Blue Cats but unfortunately no one has been able to substantiate this story. It would be fitting for Royalty to own such creatures as they are the essence of grace and good manners. We do know, however, that around the 1860s an English diplomat received one as a gift from the Tsar. These cats were reputed to be the favourites of the Russian aristocracy, so such a gift would have been considered an honour. These early cats were of the deepest blue with large ears and long heads. They steadily increased in numbers and around 1900 there are records of Russian Blues appearing at

Larry Gilbert with 'George'.

cat shows. After the Russian Revolution in 1917, it was not considered appropriate to use the term 'Russian Blue' any longer, and the name was changed to Blue Foreign Cats. By this time, the eyes of these cats had evolved into a gorgeous deep emerald green from a much paler yellowy colour of earlier days. Their development continued with the help of dedicated breeders who set out to retain all their fine characteristics, and they continued gaining strength, to the point where they were regularly seen at shows. By 1948, at the request of breeders, the name was changed back to 'Russian Blue' and the GCCF gave official recognition of the title.

The cat in the main picture on the previous page is 'Fyskez Gyorgy Szoltsany' – 'George'.

One-year-old 'George' was a best-of-breed winner in kitten classes and is looking forward to a bright future in the show ring. In the meantime he spends his time at his home in Leicestershire with his owners Anne and Larry Gilbert and their nine other Russian Blues. Typical of his breed, 'George' is very people orientated; he endears himself to everyone he meets and loves visitors who make a fuss of him, but even though he gives the impression of being the perfect gentleman, 'George' is still capable of sulking if he

From all angles – Russian Blue kittens tuck into their supper.

doesn't get his own way. He will sit with his back to Anne and Larry if he is not happy.

'George' has an amazing sense of smell, and is particularly partial to Gucci aftershave. Whenever Larry wears it, 'George' gets very excited and sniffs him all over, licking his ears and the back of his neck, purring all the time – obviously a cat with good taste.

His taste in music however, is not quite so up market. He is a dyed-in-the-wool Dire Straits fan and will remain quiet and attentive throughout an entire tape then he will meow at length until it is played over again. Playful and mischievous 'George' is still a clumsy kitten at heart and it is not unusual for him to knock ornaments from shelves as he picks his way along, whilst his older relatives are much more adept at stepping carefully. He is so clumsy that he is quite capable of dozing on some high vantage point, nodding off, and then *falling* off it, creating a constant source of amusement for Anne and Larry.

Right: Russian Blue brother and sister, 'Andrew' and 'Svetlana'.
Below: Rooftop prowl for 'Katharina'.

Siamese

It was considered fashionable for Siamese cats to grace the drawing rooms of elegant houses.

Siamese cats were introduced to the Western World well over 100 years ago and this elegant breed has steadily increased in popularity since then. How they arrived in England is uncertain, but there are records of cats of a Siamese description being shown here in London in 1871. Their appearance was apparently received with mixed feelings, some people even describing them as unnatural. There was a period around the early 1900s when it was considered fashionable for Siamese cats to grace the drawing rooms of elegant houses. I am sure that in those early days, pampered pets lived fine and comfortable lives, but there is much more to Siamese cats than being merely objects of decoration. They are vocal and highly intelligent and owners claim that they are one of the easiest breeds to train. It is not unusual to see a Siamese cat walking on a lead or sitting majestically on the back windowsill of a car (not really a safe practice but the cats seem to enjoy it).

These beautiful creatures are steeped in history, and we can really only guess as to their exact origins. Many believe that they really did exist in Siam (Thailand) many hundreds of years ago as guardians of Buddhist Temples. They were considered sacred cats who carried the souls of dead royalty on their way to the afterlife. Held in high regard by the Siamese royal family, these cats were seldom, if ever, owned by ordinary people. These ancient felines were then, as they are today, extremely elegant and beautiful, with lithe slender muscular bodies and long elegant legs, their heads forming a triangle in shape from their noses to the tips of their ears, with eyes of brilliant sapphire blue. Their short glossy coats, fine in texture and their tails, well, what can one say about a Siamese tail? Long slim and tapering, but much more than that, expressive! One is reminded of the two Siamese cats in *The Lady and the Tramp*. Walt Disney certainly did capture the characters of 'Si' and 'Am'. One can only assume that

---

The Siamese cat should be a beautifully balanced animal with head, ears and neck carried on a long svelte body, supported on fine legs and feet with a tail in proportion. The head and profile should be wedge-shaped, neither round nor pointed. The mask complete, connected by tracings with the ears (except in kittens), the eyes a clear brilliant blue; expression alert and intelligent.

Head – *Long and well proportioned, carried upon an elegant neck, with width between the ears, narrowing in perfectly straight lines to a fine muzzle, with straight profile, strong chin and level bite.*

Ears – *Rather large and pricked, wide at base.*

Eyes – *Oriental in shape and slanting towards the nose, but with width between.*

Body, Legs and Feet – *Body medium in size, long and svelte. Legs proportionately slim, hind legs slightly higher than front legs, feet small and oval. The body, legs and feet should all be in proportion, giving the whole a well balanced appearance.*

Tail – *Long and tapering, free from any kink.*

Points – *Mask, ears, feet and tail dense and clearly defined colour, matching in basic colour on all points, showing clear contrast between points and body colour. Mask complete and (except in kittens) connected by tracings with the ears.*

Coat – *Very short and fine in texture, glossy and close-lying.*

Points – *As per individual colour standards, any shading to appear on back and sides. Bib, chest and belly to be pale.*

someone from the Disney organisation spent many long hours watching Siamese cats to capture their true characteristics, and in particular the way they expressed themselves with their tails. Old Siamese (and by that I refer to Siamese cats of several generations ago) had distinct kinks in their tails. These days, such tails would

Tom Kennell with 'Penny'.

not be acceptable in the Show-ring, nor would eyes which carried a squint; both faults were once common but have now been bred out.

Several traditional stories explain why the Siamese cat had a kinky tail in the first place. One of my favourites tells of the beautiful Siamese princess who used to entrust her cat with the care of her jewellery – she would thread her rings onto its tail for safekeeping. But the shape of the cat's tail, slim and tapering, meant that the rings would constantly slide off again, so the princess tied a knot in it in order to prevent the loss of her treasures.

Another explains that the faults were caused by the cats sitting in the temples for many long and vigilant hours, their tails wrapped around the valued items they were guarding. They stared intently at the jewelled artefacts, never diverting their eyes for a moment in order to ensure their safety. Legend has it that this

devotion to duty eventually caused these guardian cats to squint and develop kinks in their tails.

The cat in the main picture on the previous page is 'Lookame Penny Lane' – 'Penny'.

Three-year-old 'Penny' is the pride and joy of her breeder Tom Kennell of Warwickshire. A beautiful Lilac Point Siamese, 'Penny' has spent time with maternal duties and does not make many visits to the shows. However she is the proud mother of several champions. Like all Siamese she is very vocal and follows Tom all over the house talking to him in a most demanding fashion whenever she wants something, and will not be quiet until she gets it! She is extremely active and likes nothing better than a mad dash all around the house, ending up on the top of the cat tree in her room. Yes, she *does* have her own room, or at least a room she shares with the rest of the household pets. A pampered puss, and quite right too!

Elegance in old age – 20-year-old 'Cindy' is still looking good.

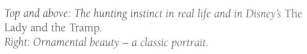

Top and above: The hunting instinct in real life and in Disney's The Lady and the Tramp.
Right: Ornamental beauty – a classic portrait.

SOMALI

Odd kittens first appeared in Abyssinian litters born in the USA.

The history of the Somali breed is fascinating. Odd kittens first appeared in Abyssinian litters born in the USA around the late 1960s. Their obvious beauty and delightful disposition inspired breeders to cultivate the type, and thus the Somali was created. It seems that the first American Somalis can be traced back to a single Abyssinian called 'Raby Chuffa', imported from England in 1957, who appears to have been carrying the long-haired gene.

The breed steadily developed in the USA and was first imported into the United Kingdom in the early 1980s. Both the Abyssinians and the Somalis have a distinctly natural look about them. Their faces have great character and with the tufts of hair on the tips of their ears, they resemble small wildcats.

Some say the Somali looks like a fox. One can understand this point of view when one takes note of their brush tails and their slinky agile bodies, but what makes the Somali so unique is its medium to long silky coat. Each hair has a base shade which is banded with a different colour. This is known as ticking. Some Somalis, in particular the ones with the longer coats, may have as many as many as twelve different bands on each hair. A breeder friend of mine likens this to the look of polished wood with a distinct grain and this is easy to see if one views these cats from above.

Nowadays these cats come in a variety of appealing shades, including soft blue and fawn or chocolate and sorrel, all beautiful and individual. Despite their wild appearance Somalis are extremely affectionate and will butt heads with anyone who will give them some time. They purr like traction engines and one owner likens

---

The overall impression of the Somali is that of a well-proportioned, medium-sized cat of foreign type, with coat of medium length, and firm, muscular development, lithe. Showing an alert, lively interest in all surroundings, with an even disposition and easy to handle. The cat is to give the appearance of activity, sound health and general vigour, with a good weight for size.

Head *– A moderate wedge, the brow, cheek and profile lines all showing a gentle contour. A slight rise from the bridge of the nose to the forehead, which should be of good size with width between the ears, flowing into the arched neck without a break. A shallow indentation forming the muzzle is desirable, but a pinch is a fault. In profile, the head shows a gentle rounding to the brow, a slight nose break is essential, leading to a firm chin. The muzzle shall not be sharply pointed and there shall be no evidence of snipiness or whisker pinch.*

Ears *– Ears set wide apart and pricked, broad at base, comparatively large, well cupped and tufted.*

Eyes *– Almond-shaped, set well apart, large, brilliant and expressive. Skull aperture neither round nor oriental. Eyes accentuated by dark lid skin, encircled by light coloured 'spectacles'. Above each eye a short dark vertical 'pencil' stroke with a dark 'pencil' line continuing from the upper lid towards the ear.*

Legs and Feet *– Legs in proportion to torso, feet oval and tufted between the toes. Five toes in front and four at the back.*

Tail *– The tail has a full brush, thick at the base and slightly tapering. Its length to balance with the torso.*

Coat *– The texture is very soft to the touch, extremely fine, dense and double-coated with at least three bands of ticking. The coat is medium length, except over the shoulders, where a shorter length is permitted. The texture and length of coat may lead to a natural separation of the fur, mainly on the chest, for which the cat should not be penalised. Preference is to be given to a cat with ruff and breeches giving a full-coated appearance to the cat.*

the sound of his cats' purr to his Harley Davidson motorbike! They actually *need* to be close to humans and are extremely sociable animals, sweet and easygoing, fitting in well with the family and any other pets which may be kept in the house.

As kittens they are pure unadulterated entertainment! They adore to be elevated and a garden is a plus for a Somali owner; climbing is a great game and one need never worry about them getting stuck up trees. I doubt if the Fire Brigade has ever been called out to rescue a Somali. This does not mean that these cats would be unhappy in an apartment, far from it. They will make their own amusement, as with the Norwegian Forest (also renowned as a tree loving cat), but adequate climbing facilities should be provided indoors.

A regular gentle nail trim at the vets or groomers will save a fortune on curtains and upholstery and the minimal fee is money well spent. A large scratching post is a must!

Somalis are reputed to be very brave, but as a general rule they are not aggressive and will only demonstrate their bravery if genuinely provoked. Somalis are not large: the males are of medium size, and females slightly smaller. This is an altogether entertaining and beautiful breed of cat and after meeting one for the first time on the photo shoot I can easily see why they are gaining in popularity.

Above: Mira Bar-Hillel with 'Sylvie'.
Below left: Looking down on the world – two young Somalis enjoy a good vantage point.
Below: Yes please! Somali kittens watch as their meal is prepared.

The cat in the main picture on page 85 is 'Chatouli Sylvie Bee' – 'Sylvie'.

As busy as a bee (hence her name), 'Sylvie' will buzz around the house, constantly on the look out for fun and mischief. This little lady demands attention and lots of physical and mental stimulation. But above all, 'Sylvie', like all Somalis, is a natural climber, and she will think nothing of scuttling up the hessian wall covering then scampering along the tops of the bookcases and down the other side only to repeat the circuit just for fun.

Wash and brush up

Rosemary Lowen has owned and bred Somalis for eight years. Her youngest cat to date is nine-month-old 'Stanley' (posh name 'Wenlo Odin'). 'Stanley' appears to all intents and purposes to be a normal friendly outgoing young Somali, but all is not what it appears to be. 'Stanley' is no ordinary cat – he cleans his own teeth!

For several weeks Rosemary was constantly picking up her husband Richard's toothbrush from the bathroom floor and replacing it into the glass by the basin. Puzzled but not particularly perturbed by this situation, Rosemary continued to retrieve the brush each day until the time came when she went into the bathroom a little earlier than usual and was surprised

Above: At the oasis – a fine example of the Somali's bushy tail.
Below: 'Stanley' cleans his teeth.

to find 'Stanley' with the brush between his front paws gnawing at the bristles with gusto. It seems that he loves the flavour of Euthymol toothpaste. Needless to say, Rosemary now keeps the bathroom door tightly closed and Richard has a brand new toothbrush.

TURKISH VAN

Cats have been living in the area around Lake Van for hundreds of years.

Pure white semi-longhaired cats have been living in the area around Lake Van in south-eastern Turkey for hundreds of years. The ones most prized by the local people have odd eyes, one green one orange, or one blue one orange, but the majority have both eyes of the same colour.

In Europe deafness is often associated with white cats, and in particular cats with blue eyes. Studies are being carried out into the reasons for this theory and to see if indeed the colour of the coat and eyes has any connection at all with deafness. It does seem that a high proportion of white cats in Europe have hearing difficulties, but in Turkey apparently this is not so – pure white Van cats have no higher incidence of deafness than cats of any other colour.

So far I have not had the opportunity to visit Turkey, but I am told by my well travelled friends that the country is absolutely fascinating, a place of contrasting cultures and beautiful scenery, large areas abundant in flora and fauna. It seems one can see storks nesting and wild tortoises, and even catch a glimpse of the occasional swimming turtle. I cannot wait to go and see it for myself; not only to experience and enjoy the surroundings and the company of the local people famous for their friendliness and hospitality, but also to visit the home of one of my favourite cats, the Turkish Van.

I have promised myself that at some time in the future I shall own one. I have a crossed-bred female, 'Sophie' featured in the Moggie section of the book, who has convinced me that she has more than a drop of Van blood in her veins (see page 62). Her sweet outgoing disposition has made her one of my all-time top cats, both for work and as a family pet. Whenever I take her to the studios, she simply strolls onto the set and takes over. She is like a little dog, outgoing and

Head – Short wedge; nose long, straight but with a barely perceptible dip in profile.

Ears – Large, well feathered, fairly close together and set high on head.

Eyes – Large and oval.

Body – Long and sturdy; the males are particularly muscular and strong.

Legs and Feet – Legs medium in length. Feet neat, well rounded and tufted.

Tail – Full brush, length to balance with the body.

Coat – Fur should be long, soft and silky to the roots. No woolly undercoat. It should be noted that the winter coat of the Van is longer and heavier than the summer coat.

friendly and amazingly intelligent; furthermore she has a fascination with water. All of these characteristics are typical of the pure bred Turkish Van Cat.

The first Van Cats imported into this country were brought over by two ladies, Sonia Halliday and Laura Lushington, in the 1950s, and the breed as we know it is said to stem directly from these. The cats of Van are semi-longhaired and predominantly white with thick bushy tails. The auburn markings on the ears and

Geoffrey Addison and Mira Bar-Hillel with 'Emma' and her son 'Boychik'.

body and in particular the tail appear only occasionally in the cats born in Turkey but have been developed by the breeders here in Europe and also in the USA. Auburn is the term used by Turkish Van people (you and I might say 'ginger'); these cats have most attractive markings, their faces are usually highly photogenic.

The cat in the main picture on the previous page is 'Chantrymere Coppelia' – 'Emma'.

'Emma' is four years old and the first pure bred Van to take over the home of Mira Bar-Hillel and her husband Geoffrey Addison who live in South West London.

Mira had decided some twelve years previously to eventually share her home with a Turkish Van after meeting one in a pub whilst on holiday in St Austell,

Cornwall. The hostelry was renowned for its steak and kidney pie, and hungry Mira had ordered a large portion. As the food was served a fluffy white cat with auburn markings strolled into the bar and jumped up onto Mira's chair. More than a little concerned with the situation, Mira was afraid that this pretty creature would put its feet onto the table or even try to eat her lunch. How wrong could she be! Van cats *never* steal food. The cat simply purred gently and curled up in her lap, totally ignoring the delicious pie. When she had finished eating, Mira and the cat became better acquainted and within minutes it was love. Told that this delightful creature was a pure-bred Turkish Van, Mira was enchanted and decided there and then that one day she would have one of her own. 'Emma' is the fulfilment of that promise.

Typical of the Van breed, 'Emma' is fun-loving, intelligent, extremely agile and playful. As her owner says, who needs television when one can be entertained

by watching a Turkish Van cavorting and chasing imaginary mice and birds? Van cats are renowned for their tolerance of water. They are known to swim in the shallows of Lake Van – but probably only in the summer months when the temperature is kind. They may not wish to dive into an icy fishpond in England! Van cats are fascinated with garden hoses and dripping taps. 'Emma' can leap up to three feet high to catch soap bubbles and she loves to sit on the side of her owners' bath tub and dip her paws into the warm water. (Perhaps Mira should give 'Emma' a rubber duck for a Christmas present?)

Mira and Geoffrey have a Van-loving friend, a jolly, quite portly middle-aged man, who recently went to his doctor for a general check up. Examining his back, the doctor made some wry comments about the gentleman's obviously exciting sex life. Puzzled at first, the patient asked what had inspired such a question, whereupon the doctor jokingly made reference to the long scratch-marks down his back (apparently with more than a little envy!). Mira's friend laughed out loud and replied, 'Wishful thinking! It's my Turkish Van Cat, he jumps onto my shoulders whenever I take a shower.'

'Emma' has produced three litters of lovely kittens and Mira and Geoffrey now have their own breed prefix, 'Chatouli'.

Above: A refreshing dip in the family pool for this Turkish Van.
Left, below and right: Made for the camera – these three kittens prove the point.

ITALIAN STREET CAT

A KITTEN WITH TRUE GRIT

'Speranza' is a moggie in a million.

I make no apologies for dedicating a whole section of this book to 'Speranza'. 'Speranza' is a moggie in a million. She belongs to my friend and valued client Julian Birri, whose home is in Milan, Italy. Julian is an advertising agency producer and we have often worked together filming TV commercials for the Italian market. It was on such an occasion that we were shooting in London with my young dog 'Pippin Junior' making a film to promote Italian slippers. During a break in filming, Julian and I chatted about my forthcoming book and, as he is a dedicated cat lover, I asked him if he had any interesting stories to tell; it was then that I learned of 'Speranza'. I am honoured that Julian has allowed me to publish her story, a fitting tribute to (as Julian says) a kitten with true grit, and of course, to Julian and his wife Susanna, who have opened their home and their hearts to a permanently disabled little cat who will require constant love and attention for the rest of her life.

On 5 August 1994, Julian Birri and his wife were coming up off a rocky beach on Elba. They saw a group of people looking down at something and shaking their heads. The 'something' turned out to be a really pitiful sight – a tiny kitten, crawling in the hot sun, tongue hanging out from thirst, dragging its back legs and covered in flies.

They picked her up, wrapped her in a beach towel and drove home, where they gave her water and a jar of baby food they'd bought, all of which was greedily and gratefully devoured. They then washed her back (they'd found out that she was a girl) but could discover no wounds. Her back legs didn't work at all, but she seemed to feel no pain. The obvious thing to be done was go to a vet, but it was too late in the evening. So they put her in the guest bathroom with several towels on the floor, a bowl of water and let her rest for the night. From time to time they peeped in and saw she was sound asleep.

At six next morning Julian was awakened by an unaccustomed sound he can only describe as loud cheeping. It turned out to be their guest, sturdily requesting breakfast. She polished off more baby food and milk, then took great interest in what their other five cats and three dogs were eating.

Off they went to the vet, an energetic and enthusiastic young optimist called Luigi Corbelli, who gave the kitten a thorough going over and pronounced she must have been run over by a bicycle or a moped, but was in no apparent pain. However, as there was no x-ray equipment available, it was impossible to know what her internal situation really was. Should he put her to sleep painlessly there and then or were they willing to give her a chance, knowing they might have to put her down later? The answer came from the kitten who let out a vigorous 'cheep'! The vet laughed and said, 'She sounds

Julian Birri with 'Speranza'.

lively enough, and as long as there's life, there's hope!' Julian and Susanna walked out of the vet's surgery with a chirping kitten who now had a name – 'Speranza', which in Italian means hope.

The next weeks were fascinating. Initially they kept 'Speranza' in a large cage when outdoors, so that she would feel part of daily activities, and from time to time

the nickname 'Pigola', which is Italian for the sound chicks make.

Back in Milan they had her examined by the very best vet, who did an x-ray and confirmed that her spine had been damaged, and could in no way be operated upon. His honest advice was to put her to sleep.

By then, of course, neither Julian nor Susanna

they let her move around freely on a large, danger-free terrace. Far from crawling, she began to skitter around, playing with the other cats' tails, basking in the sunshine, and sleeping curled up against their largest dog, a kind-hearted and somewhat bewildered giant called 'Bendico'.

At mealtimes they would put the cage on a chair next to the table, where 'Speranza' would continually ask for food in such an insistent 'cheep' that she got

wanted to do that. Seeing how cheerfully 'Speranza' took her disablement, how much energy and liveliness she put into everything she did, they decided that somewhere in the world someone must have had a similar problem, and solved it. After some research, they got in touch with Dianne Barrow in the UK, who represents an American company specialising in making carts for disabled animals. Yes, they could make a cart for 'Speranza', just send her weight and measurements. They did, and a month later the cart arrived. They adjusted it to 'Speranza's' exact measurements, carefully strapped her in and put her on the floor.

After a moment of puzzlement she took a step forward. Then two, then three and suddenly – *whizz* – she went flying through the house. The other cats jumped up in amazement as the 'ugly duckling' went supersonic. She soon got another nickname, 'Ben Hur', as she blithely ran her cart over everything, including the feet of anyone in her way.

It took her no time at all to learn the tricks of the cart. She now goes backwards and sideways, and can turn more tightly than a London taxi, sensing exactly which furniture is too low for her to go under, and which gap is too narrow to pass through.

Julian and Susanna have added a little bell to the cart so that they can hear where she is, and a sanitary napkin on the back because she doesn't always have control over her rear end. During the day she contentedly snoozes in her cart, simply resting her front half on a cushion. At night they put her in a nappy (Pampers for girls to be precise) and she romps around in that before going to bed.

So, touching wood, 'Speranza' today is a healthy, sturdy, cheerful and rather spoilt young lady. She has a hearty appetite, and insists on being put onto the breakfast table, cart and all so that she can watch them eat. She plays with a special friend, one of the other cats called 'Conte Zio', who has adopted her and washes her every morning and night.

Problems? A few, now and then. Occasionally she has trouble digesting, travelling in a car sometimes makes her sick, and of course, she needs constant care and attention. But she's worth it all. She only has to see someone coming to visit and she starts purring at full volume. If they pick her up they get an immediate lick on the nose. Her conversation has progressed from simple cheeping to a whole vocabulary.

'Speranza' now has a new fibreglass cart, in Ferrari red, specially designed and built by two generous lunatics who produce special effects for TV and the cinema. This 'racing model' is ultra-light, easier to put on and keep clean, and more comfortable to doze in.

In conclusion Julian and Susanna Birri would like to thank a whole lot of people who have gone out of their way to help a rather sickly and disabl d kitten to enjoy life as a fairly normal cat. If anybody reading this has similar problems they would be more than happy to help and advise. 'Arthur' knows how to find them.

Her Ferrari-red cart is no problem to 'Speranza'. Hunting snoozing or strolling, anything is possible.

ALL GOOD THINGS COME TO AN END

The old cat may well have stepped down from public duties by the time this book is published. A tough act to follow, he has performed like a consummate professional throughout his entire career.

Never once has he faltered or put a paw wrong in the nine years that he has been representing his favourite brand of catfood. I can honestly say with my hand on my heart that 'Arthur' has been a joy to work with from day one. He has always behaved like a perfect gentleman.

Now the time has come for him to 'put his paws up' and take it easy. There is a youngster waiting in the wings to take over the role, and by an incredible coincidence he is yet another 'Snowy' from The Wood Green Animal Shelter!

The dynasty lives on.